Auschwitz Sur
Survived Hit

By Pastor Survivor

American History X Editor
World War 2 Publishing
Holocaust Photos Illustrator

All Rights Reserved. No part of this publication may be reproduced in any form, by any means, including scanning, photocopying, or otherwise without the prior written consent from the copyright holder. Special Amazon Edition 2015

Copyright

Chapter 1

Introduction: A Prayer For Unity and Healing

"God lift up the countless victims who were sacrificed to the Moloch of
War and to the millions of survivors uprooted from their native soil whose ultimate fate rests in the benign hands of the Divine Providence. May their sufferings appease the just wrath of an all Holy Deity and may they bring mankind true peace and a sense of universal brotherhood."

Introduction

Many impressive books have been written about German horror camps where, from 1939 until 1945, human beings were subjected to degrading experiences, or were destroyed like swarms of helpless insects.

Every publisher in the U.S.A. has been offered at least one hair-raising diary, and the flow of these human stories will probably continue for many years to come. It would seem to be a sign of mass psychosis. Former inmates of concentration camps have to tell their story. And many people feel reluctant to read another book filled with the smoke of burned bodies.

Morbid or not, it is indeed a strong urge that prompts those who escaped from hell to tell the world about it.

Remember Job:

"Who will grant me that they (my words) be marked down in a book with an iron pen and in a plate of lead, or be graven with a graver on the flint stone?" (Job 19, 23-24)

The modern Job who has spent five or more years in a horror camp has indeed a story to tell, if only to stir human conscience and show the wickedness of modem man who refused to worship God but made a pact with the Devil.

The camp where I stayed for several years has received less publicity than the larger and more smoothly run DACHAU and RAVENSBRUCK camps where mass extermination was carried out with cold efficiency.

Our camp was called BRZEZINSKI, in German BIRKENAU. Some prisoners nicknamed it RAJSKO. In literal translation this means "HEAVENLIKE".

In Brzezinski - Birkenau, mass murder was carried out on such a fantastic scale that the executioners had set up five crematories. Almost all the inmates were destroyed and only a few lived long enough to greet their liberators. Except for one book written by a Polish woman thus far, no report has been graved on flint stone by any of the liberated Polish Jobs.

I am not a writer and my story will be a plain and frank account of things which I have witnessed and experienced in nine prisons and in three concentration camps, from which I was miraculously saved by God. It is not my aim to evoke your pity, nor to arouse your wrath against the Germans. I wish only to help you to realize what happens when man rejects God and when his passions become his sole master. He will then commit every kind of inhuman crime, whereas if he follows the Golden Rule he will withstand the most ruthless pressure and even in the midst of inhuman sufferings will desperately cling to his faith.

I wish to stir the conscience of statesmen so that they may unify their efforts in preventing a repetition of the crimes committed in the name of an omnipotent and evil deity — the STATE.

Pastor, Author

Chapter 2

My Fifth Prison

"Prisoners Are Not Allowed to Look Through the Window..."

I did not pay attention to the stern warning. The window became the only attractive spot in the dreary prison cell.

The window collaborated with the prisoners...

It showed us pictures, it disclosed various scenes.

In winter we saw only a blanket of snow and the dark silhouettes of naked trees. Crows circled in the mist. Nothing seemed to happen on the bleak stage. But nevertheless I could look at it for hours.

The window was like a little door inviting us for a stroll, at least in spirit. All prisoners felt the same.

In the KALISZ prison we had to place chairs one on top of another and to climb on them like circus clowns. Some prisoners used to climb on the water pipe connected with the toilet. At least once a day each one of us had to look through the window.

In SIERADZ — the window showed a more varied landscape: two railway tracks and a long, winding line of trains and passenger cars filled with soldiers; freight cars loaded with war material; cars, bearing the Red Cross, carried the wounded.

In our cell crammed with men who waited for trial or for the signal to depart to a death camp, the air was heavy with the sickening smell of damp clothes and unwashed bodies.

We knew that somewhere on the white Russian steppes the war was raging. Dead and wounded soldiers were lying in the cold embrace of a terrible Russian winter. German guards often talked about that Russian winter. They were obviously afraid of being sent to the dreaded Eastern front. It had become a kind of obsession.

Forgetting the rules, they also looked through the window and stared with blinking unbelieving eyes at the ambulance trains, which bore the Red Cross on each car. These cars appeared more and more often. They came from the East. They seemed to multiply. And the guards looked more and more gloomy.

I remember when the news of the war with Russia spread like fire, a new hope seemed to light up the dark cells of the Kalisz prison.

During the daily stroll in the yard I could not refrain from smiling at the sight of one of the officials. His beefy face looked so harassed and dazed. He flew into a rage. He slapped me on the face and kicked me several times. I wonder where he is now. He must have changed his job. There are no jobs in Birkenau for German guards any more.

After two years I had a record of four prisons. Then I landed in the fifth one.

Old timers used to tell me that the first days are the most crucial for every newcomer. One cannot get used to the thought of being locked up. Later on, however, the craving for freedom becomes less acute and one begins to get used to the new surroundings. This is exactly how I felt.

When the Gestapo caught me in Sanok, I found myself in the local prison. This first prison was not too bad, though. The cell was almost comfortable. In spite of this, each day seemed to last a year and I suffered like a wild animal trapped by hunters. At the thought of a long imprisonment, I would break out in a cold sweat which made me shiver.

Gradually, however, I became less impatient.

The dreadful, dismal and degrading prisons of Lodz, Cracow and Kalisz could not deprive me of a certain newly acquired indifference. I was more and more detached and calm. The slamming of iron and wooden gates of every new prison failed to impress me, though quite often my heart would bolt like a frightened fox.

My trial took place in Kalisz. I had to walk to the courtroom through a lovely city park. The way was familiar to me as I had often trodden the same soft path, amid the old trees and flowerbeds. I never guessed that a few years later I would have to follow it as a prisoner of the German Gestapo.

A group of children recognized me. They disappeared like a flock of birds, probably to notify my friends. When I was leaving the court, I saw them again waiting for me with a crowd of people. I recognized many old friends and neighbors. Their wistful but smiling faces made me feel happy.

The prosecutor did not spare words in condemning and vilifying the anti-German attitude of the Polish intellectuals. I was sentenced to four years of hard labor.

The decision of the court did not shock me, as I had already spent two years in various prisons. The only important thing was the war. How and when would it end? It was the war and not the German prosecutors which would have the last word.

In 1942 Hitler still believed in his "star". As for us, since we did not believe in his invincibility, all of us patiently waited for the day when Hitler's star would be put out by the victors.

In Sieradz the stillness of the night was sometimes shattered by the screaming warning of antiaircraft sirens. The shrill whining was followed by a thunder of motors.

"That's nothing ... Just an English plane," explained the guards.

When the noise subsided, the silence became unbearable. It was most discouraging. A good thunderbolt falling right in the midst of us would have been an answer to our prayers. It would at least announce that a real counteroffensive had begun. "When will the Allies begin to pound Germany with real bombs?" prisoners were asking one another. But days and weeks passed by and nothing happened. However we had one consolation. Cars with the Red Cross became more numerous, and eventually no other trains appeared on the horizon.

Liberation?

In 1942 the prison of Sieradz was crammed to capacity. In three blocks, where there was space for only 600 men, 4,000 prisoners had to live together. Small cells intended for five people had 52 tenants. Food was becoming scarce. Many prisoners developed dropsy, others became tubercular. One day when we felt hopeless and doomed, the guards announced a new regulation. Orders had come from Berlin. All prisoners who had been sentenced to more than three years would be liberated immediately. They would finish their sentence after the war was over. Lack of space — don't you know. Prisoners cannot become a burden to the Almighty State.

The news spread like fire. Some prisoners would not believe it, others went wild with joyful expectation.

When the first group was "liberated" a few days later, some doubts were expressed by those who saw them handed over to a detachment of German policemen, who escorted them to the railway station.

"Where did they go? Somewhere, to be sure."

Another convoy was organized the following week. Every prisoner had an identification card with the following information: "Released from the prison of on the. Handed over to the Gestapo".

Many prisoners objected to leaving the prison, but they had no choice.

Convoys left Sieradz and Lodz, Warsaw and Cracow. Thousands of men and women were released and sent "somewhere" in special trains. We learned later that German SS-men were rounding up hundreds of men in restaurants, in stores, in churches and in the streets. Many had been dragged during the night from their homes. They were taken prisoner and led away in their nightclothes.

I learned subsequently that a stream of trucks and cars was proceeding in the direction of the concentration camps of Majdanek, Oswiecim, Dachau and Sachsenhausen. When my turn came I did not know where my journey would end, but I remember that I prayed to God not to be sent to Oswiecim.

On January 15, 1943, 628 of us waited in the prison yard for the departure signal. One hundred armed policemen surrounded us and one of them shouted angrily: "The first man who makes a move will be shot".

It was 8 P.M. when the gates of the prison opened with a screeching noise.

The Germans liked to do their evil work during the night.

The night became their accomplice. It was the best time for every kind of evil: executions, searching parties, rounding up of innocent victims. After curfew when a Pole was not allowed to be in the streets, gangs of young Hitlerites desecrated small chapels and wayside shrines. They broke the beautiful wooden crosses on the highways and in the market places. During the night, too, they carried away their spoils and transported looted treasures.

It was a starless night when they arrested me in Sanok. Our Franciscan monastery and the church in Kalisz were searched by German policemen after midnight. Four brothers and one priest kidnapped by SS-men died later in a concentration camp.

In the prison of Kalisz, twice at 3 A.M. we heard a roll call of prisoners sentenced to death.

On one night a group of helpless victims was loaded in a van and sent to the woods. I will never forget that terrible night. I remember some of the names: Maksymilian Niewiadomski, Ciesielski, Joseph Szymanski... A witness who was later released told me how they were ordered to kneel down in front of a ditch, and were shot in the back of the head.

In Kalisz, Father Pawlowski was publicly executed on the Square of Liberty. Such shows were unusual; the Germans preferred to do their work behind the black curtain of the night.

It was also during the night that the prisoners were questioned by Gestapo torturers. During my short stay in the Cracow prison of Monteluppi I met a young girl, a student of a Cracow college. A Gestapo man was doing his best to make her betray her friends. He was courteous and kind while he tempted her with a promise of special privileges. The girl was adamant. She would not answer any questions. Just as I entered the room one of the agents of the Gestapo made an insulting remark. I had my Franciscan habit on me. He grabbed my cord and my rosary and jeered: "You could use them as a noose. The cord is strong enough."

The girl could not stand it, she burst into tears. One of the men took a white chalk and drew a cross on my back, another German called a guard and ordered him to escort me to the railway station.

All these memories are still haunting me and I often get lost in day dreaming about the horrible past.

It was during a stormy night that I was "released" from the prison of Sieradz. We were a crowd of 628 men escorted by armed policemen.

In spite of the darkness I noticed the ghastly pallor of my frightened colleagues. When we boarded the train, no one knew where we were going. A few hours later someone whispered in my ear: "We just passed Lodz. The train is going to the East"."

For Heaven's sake, can it be that we are being sent to Oswiecim?"

Oswiecim, or Auschwitz, won the doubtful honor of being THE horror camp and its name alone had an ominous portent.

We did not sleep. We did not feel like talking, surrounded by armed guards who paced the cars all the time."

Are you a priest?" I heard a voice coming from nowhere. Startled I turned my head. A German guard was standing behind me.

"Yes, I am."

"Did you say Mass today?" he inquired. He stared at me intently and then, without waiting for a reply, quickly went away.

I never saw him again, but I do not doubt that he was at heart tired and disgusted. He did not have the courage to rebel, but he had enough decency to send to me a small package of tobacco through Section of the concentration camp at Oswiecim — Auschwitz. Another prisoner. Auschwitz

The train stopped for a few minutes at Czestochowa, the Polish Lourdes. At dawn we saw the tall chimneys of Silesian iron works. The stations now had strange

German names, distorted translations of historic Polish names.

The dreaded word AUSCHWITZ appeared on posters and on walls. The train was now running on a new sidetrack. It stopped abruptly.

I gasped. It was Auschwitz.

In this flat country a ghost town made of barracks seemed to rise from the soil. It was Brzezinki-Birkenau an annex of the ill-famed Oswiecim (Auschwitz) camp.

Memories of days gone by come back to me. I was a boy of seventeen. I had just graduated from high school and my only desire was to become a Franciscan monk. The call was so strong that immediately upon receiving the invitation from the Franciscan Fathers, I left my native Zoltaniec, near Lwow, and started on the journey.

From Lwow to Lagiewniki the way is long and rather tedious, but I was carried on the wings of my heart's desire.

I was bent on abandoning the world and entering a closed monastery where I would feel nearer to God in an atmosphere of contemplation and prayer.

When I stepped off the train I did not even notice the weight of a heavy basket on my arm which my good mother had filled with food. I almost ran up the mountain but was stopped by a big dog.

I looked around me. On the green meadows several cows were grazing and a tall shepherd stood near by. He was reciting his rosary. It was one of the brothers. How I wanted to be like him, free and detached from the world and close to God; I almost danced when I rang the bell of the Monastery.

Several years later, on January 16, 1943 after two years of imprisonment. I was standing in front of another gate. This was indeed the gate of hell.

Oswiecim, or Auschwitz, won notoriety from the very day of its opening.

Since 1940 it had been nothing else but a slaughterhouse for millions of prisoners.

There was not a single household in Poland where at least one person was not acquainted with Oswiecim. This monstrous trap seemed to swallow its victims. One entered it to disappear forever. After many months relatives usually received a short message, bearing the seal with the swastika and announcing the death "from natural causes" of Number...

"Nr (first name and surname followed) died of a heart attack. You may apply for his ashes.

No one ever believed the German obituaries. We know too well what was going on inside of the camp. One or two prisoners who bribed their way back to freedom told the truth. Inebriated SS-men used to boast of the efficiency of the methods applied at Oswiecim.

A teacher whom I met near Sanok in 1941 would not speak about his experiences in Oswiecim from which he miraculously escaped, but he pointed a finger to his head covered with horrible scars. He added: "When I entered Oswiecim I weighed two hundred pounds. I was a big, husky man. Look at me now. I am a hopeless wreck, a prematurely aged man good for nothing".

He did not enjoy his freedom much longer, but died six months later.

As far back as 1941, we all knew what Oswiecim was like, and that is why I deliberately chose four years of prison by pleading guilty to the charge of having listened to foreign broadcasts. The judge had no satisfactory evidence of my guilt but I hastened to say "yes". I knew that I could stand prison even for five years but that I would succumb very quickly to the Oswiecim regime. And that is where they would have sent me as a suspect whose guilt not been sufficiently substantiated. A concentration camp would crush the resistance of any suspect.

But only God knew what was lying in store for me. The prison was only a beginning, a stepping-stone that would lead me to Oswiecim — Brzezinki.

Oswiecim – Auschwitz

Oswiecim is an old Polish town. In 1939 it had about 5,000 inhabitants. It is situated in a valley near Czechoslovakia, at a distance of 30 miles from the historic city of Cracow. The narrow Sola River, a branch of the beautiful Vistula, runs through the desolate marshland. The climate is unhealthy. The weather changes during the day. Heavy mists overhanging the swamps are often chased by violent gales. Malaria is rampant.

Centuries ago the little town was the capital of an independent principality of the Dukes of Oswiecim. In their wildest dreams they did not foresee that it would become a horror camp, set up by a nation that boasted of its magnificent culture.

The Germans at first organized a camp in some barracks near the railway station. However in 1940 they had to put up annexes for an unending procession of prisoners.

On the 15th of August, which is the anniversary of the "Miracle of the Vistula" of 1920 (Poland at that time repelled a Bolshevik invasion), the Germans organized a manhunt through the streets of Warsaw. At least 1600 victims were sent to Oswiecim. The camp, crammed to overflowing, had to be enlarged. Prisoners were promptly put to work, goaded on by clubs and whips, which proved excellent weapons in the hands of supervisors.

Men and women worked at terrific speed. The many who died on the spot from overexertion were immediately replaced by others.

In the beginning prisoners died not only from overwork.

Hunger took its toll slowly but relentlessly.

Lack of sanitary facilities in filthy dormitories had created an ideal breeding ground for every kind of germ. But even germs were less efficient than the SS-men who killed their victims with obvious delight. The rattling of machine guns or sudden bursts of shots were heard at night and almost every day. We lived in constant fear.

One day we saw a group of forty young women before the main entrance.

Someone made the remark that they were students from Cracow. We entered our cells and a few hours later we heard the rattling of a machine gun.

Then — silence. A deadly silence for about ten minutes.

After a while, a military truck appeared on the main street of the camp. It was covered with gray tarpaulin. Some dark liquid was trickling from under the cover, leaving large red spots on the dusty road. A detachment of prisoners stared at the truck, but they were sharply reprimanded and ordered to leave as quickly as possible.

When evening came, two prisoners were sent with pails full of sand, and were told to spread it on the bloody spots.

One of my colleagues had once witnessed an execution.

He saw it through a hole in a wooden partition. Victims waited in a line. The first victim, an old man with a swollen face, walked to a pillar on the border of a deep trench. SS-men aimed at him. My friend heard a shot. Than the man toppled into the ditch. Promptly the next prisoner followed him, then a third one. One after another they disappeared into the trenches. The guards would not waste bullets. Only one to each victim. It was all done quickly and efficiently like in a show, where you can't miss the target. The only difference was that instead of gay music the air was filled with the screams and moans of the dying who wanted to settle some old accounts with the world.

In the spring of 1941, the Camp had developed into a fairly large settlement; but while it spread all over the country like a monstrous trap it could not accommodate the thousands of newcomers arriving every day.

The German commanders decided to set up three new annexes. One of them became the famous camp of BRZEZINKI — BIRKENAU. Birke means a birch tree. (The Polish name Brzezinki — is a derivative from Brzezina — a birch tree.)

Brzezinki — Birkenau

In January of 1943 the convoy sent from the prison of Sieradz was on its way to Birkenau. The camp was situated at a distance of two miles from Oswiecim.

I imagine that before the German invasion the countryside must have been as lovely as all such spots in Poland are. Though damp and muddy, it had a peculiar charm. Green lanes buzzed with life. Wild ducks swarmed above the streams and marshes. In May, picturesque groups of peasants sang hymns beside wayside shrines with their wooden crosses and statues of the Holy Virgin and the patron saints.

There was a lot of music in the air, and at nightfall you could hear the croaking of frogs and the metallic buzzing of grasshoppers. Before sunrise, lonely hunters crossed the marshland teeming with wild birds. In winter, all the ponds and brooks were covered with ice, providing a playground for children.

In spite of the unhealthy climate, people liked their homes and felt happy.

No one guessed that one day Oswiecim would become a symbol of hell.

After the German invasion of Poland, the scenery changed promptly. Instead of farms and barns, crumbling walls spared by fire and lonely chimneys pointed their scorched arms to the sky. Broken wayside crosses lay in the dust. Holy statues lay shattered in pieces. There were no sounds of human voices, no songs, no laughter, only the lament of frogs and the nostalgic cry of wild ducks.

Within a radius of several miles, a monstrous prison camp rose in the valley with a large morgue, five crematories and two stakes at which the dead were burned.

The camp of Birkenau had been set up in 1941.

One day a group of SS-officers arrived in military cars. They spent several hours travelling across the country, through fields and meadows. It looked like a searching party. Then they disappeared.

A few days later, a company of prisoners was brought from Oswiecim and some kind of work was started in the swamps.

At the same time, all the inhabitants for 25 miles around ordered to leave their homes at once. The order was strict. Everyone had to abandon his dwelling. Eventually another battalion of slave workers began to tear down all the buildings.

In no time the first barracks, made of wood and cement, appeared on the scene. Those made of wooden logs had the shape of large stables.

When I arrived in Birkenau two years later, in 1943, there were about 14,000 prisoners.

It is worth mentioning that the Germans usually chose such regions for prison camps as could not be exploited for other uses: marshland, sandy soil unfit for cultivation, mountainsides. Unhealthy spots had priority. This was in accordance with the Nazi ideology and with the program of extermination "at the lowest possible cost" of those elements that had no value for the Reich.

In comparison with other prisons, particularly with that of Monteluppi in Cracow, Birkenau was appallingly filthy.

In Monteluppi, which was an ancient military prison, conditions were different. It was a regular prison, such as might be found in any European country.

The Germans of course introduced their own methods.

During my stay there, I witnessed a "show" which at that time did not give me any clue as to what would happen to me in the future.

In the big yard I saw prisoners standing in groups of four, with their faces turned to the wall. Some prisoners had a cross drawn with white chalk on their backs. I noticed that three or four men had an interrogation point while others had a circle instead of a cross. They all were deadly pale and stood motionless like wooden puppets. I counted about 600 men. Several SS-guards were shooting in various directions with guns and pistols.

I later learned that the majority of these prisoners would be sent to the horror camp of Birkenau, others to Oswiecim, and one group to some unknown destination.

They had to stand and wait for hours. No one was allowed to turn his head. They heard the noise of shooting, and each wondered when a bullet aimed at him would stop the sinister show. But that was not an execution; it was only one of the favorite games organized by SS-men, who delighted in scaring the wits out of their captives. In Birkenau my first impression was that of incredible filth.

Prisoners were so ragged and dirty that their faces had the color of slate.

In the barrack yards and trenches heaps of stinking rags and rubbish were piled up. Along the barbed wire enclosure mountains of refuse were continuously burned and a foul smelling smoke spread over the area. Its acrid odor made one cough and choke.

At first I would not believe that people could stay longer than a few days in such dismal surroundings. But soon I discovered that man is a tougher and more resistant creature than a cat or a horse. He is able to withstand experiences that would kill a bull.

No. 88092

In every camp and in every prison the newcomer had to undergo a routine checkup.

Your clothes were taken away by an official, then you were sent to a barbershop where you got a close hair cut. After this, your head looked like a golf ball. A thorough disinfection took care of possible insects. A hot and cold bath made you feel happy for a short while.

Then you were registered. You lost your name and you got a number. Your pedigree was hereafter to be looked for only in the prison's register. Your coat of arms was stamped on your arm.

My turn came after three hours of waiting. We were quite a crowd. From time to time an old prisoner would approach us stealthily and beg for a piece of bread or for some clothes.

Others behaved differently. They walked with an assured look, gave orders, escorted prisoners and you could guess at a glance that they already became part of the administration.

One of them approached us and shouted at the top of his voice:

All athletes and former cops step out."

No one seemed to understand the strange order. We did not know that all heavy and light athletes and former policemen were enrolled among the personnel of the camp. Their task was to destroy their own comrades.

In the immediate neighborhood of the barracks where we had to wait, we saw a long shed. One part of it was so close to us that we could look through the disjointed planks into a dark room. Some daring men were already peeping into the shed. I joined them.

When my eyes grew used to the darkness I saw naked bodies piled up, or spread on the floor. Bodies covered with bluish spots. Others disfigured, with horrible wounds, and splashed with blood.

I felt a cold shiver along my head. For the first time in my life I experienced the feeling, so often described in fairy tales, of having my hair stand on my head.

There was no time to meditate on the lot of the unfortunate victims of Nazism. I was ordered to enter the store with clothes. I was naked, as I gave up all my clothes before taking a bath. That communal bath was a dreadfully cold place. Icicles hung around the faucets and white frost decorated the walls. From heaps of used garments in the shed I received a pair of trousers made of ticking and a blouse. Some lucky men succeeded in obtaining a dirty undershirt.

As soon as my family name was written in the registry, an expert in tattooing took hold of my arm. The operation lasted only two minutes.

In the space of two minutes I got rid of my family record. I became a Number.

From then on I would be known only as Number 88092.

During roll calls I would have to be careful not to forget that I was no more a Franciscan Father but Number 88092.

Whenever I had to report, I would have to mention only the Number. Anyway it was easy to remember: they printed it on each piece of my clothing.

After my liberation I vainly tried to get rid of it. It was so deeply ingrained that I will have to carry it until the very end.

One Day's Toll

Chapter 3

A Slow Stoll To Hell

In normal life no one is safe from unexpected mishaps. Even those who are sheltered and protected may become victims of accidents. Newspapers are filled with descriptions of such misfortunes Workers get trapped in a mine. People die crushed by their own trucks. Lumberjacks are often hurt by falling trees. Housewives break their necks on the floor of their kitchens.

The victim of an accident is an object of compassion. Ambulances and doctors rush to help. Hospitals are ready for emergency cases. Relatives try to console him, and for a while the entire world seems to bend with a sympathetic smile upon the unfortunate victim.

In the German horror camps things were slightly different.

Newcomers had to undergo quarantine. After ten days they were assigned to bunks in a block, and were sent to work.

Our block, Number 16, was sent to the labor camp for the first time on a windy day. Besides shirt and trousers each prisoner was given a light coat and a cap.

When our column left the camp a band was playing a German military march.

Our assignment was to prepare the grounds for a new barrack.

We had to remove heaps of ice and snow, then to dig into the frozen earth with heavy picks and to cart the load away.

Newcomers not yet completely worn out moved quickly, dug and chopped with all their strength and carted their load at a great speed, but they grew tired fast. Only then they got their first lesson in good behavior. They realized that it is better to spare one's energy and not to spend it during the first hours than to feel the impact of a club on one's back when trying to rest for a minute. Each prisoner was expected to work continuously and without slowing down.

Guards chosen from old timers, mostly criminals, called KAPO, watched us like hawks.

The slightest change in the attitude of the slave was noticed and punished with painful blows. Anyway, one had to move, quickly because of the bitter frost. Overalls made of ticking; a light coat and torn shoes without socks are a poor protection against cold.

By nine o'clock in the morning we were already exhausted. Many felt drowsy and had dizzy spells. About noon they were unable to move and collapsed in the snow, the heavy picks rolling from their numb hands. Even the wild shouting and cursing of the Kapo proved a futile stimulus.

Like dry leaves falling from a tree swept by winter gales many of my comrades died during the work.

It is strange how happy they looked when, overcome by fatigue, they just fell on the ground and lay in the snow, seemingly peaceful and completely relaxed: young men with a healthy appearance, killed by overexertion and by the frost, old men, who did not need much to finish them off, the thread of their lives having been cut.

No one was allowed to take care of them. At the end of the day a special detail would gather the dead and the dying and carry them to the camp. O yes; living and dead "had to register" during the roll call.

A shrill sound of whistles announced the end of our working day. The work had started at seven; we carried on until four, with fifteen minutes of rest for a non-existent lunch. Our only meal was a cup of weak black coffee and a piece of stale bread in the morning before leaving camp.

The Prisoners formed a long procession.

Dead and dying men, a total of forty on the first day, were placed on low sledges...

The wind carried an echo of cheerful tunes played by the camp orchestra.

It was the "hello" sent by hell to those rehiring to its depths. But the moans of the dying, now brought back to consciousness for a short while by a horrible fear of being buried together with the dead, sounded louder than the music.

The living men lying among the corpses vainly endeavored to push their way to the border of the sledges. They gasped for lack of air. No one came to their rescue.

The guards did not even look at the moving hearse. They were too busy watching the living.

At the gates of the camp a band greeted us with a loud and triumphal march. SS-guards began to count the columns. Reports concerning casualties were received with a grin.

Our Kapo reported: "Forty dead and sick on sledges". "Very well," snapped the SS-man. "Rotten pigs. That's what they are. And the sooner we get rid of them, the better."

Each battalion of slave workers was followed by a sledge or a truck filled up with bodies and with the sick. Later on, when we did not have enough trucks to cart them back, stronger prisoners had to carry the bodies on their shoulders.

Even when winter had passed and spring brought milder weather, the number of casualties was as great as ever. Those who could stand the frost were killed by guards for the slightest insubordination. Whenever an SS-man noticed any slackening of work, at least one man had to pay for it with his life. Prisoners were either shot or beaten to death or drowned. Many were strangled by sadistic Kapos.

I myself saw an SS-man killing a prisoner with his club. He crushed the head of the unfortunate fellow, who had slipped in the mud while dragging a heavy bag of cement.

On other occasions I saw people murdered, because they went a few yards away from the spot assigned to them. Others died because they approached a fire and tried to warm their hands. One man was killed because he stayed too long in the latrine.

I would not be able to count all the blows I got, while working on the construction of an artificial pond. The mud was loaded on stretcher-like carriers and we were ordered to walk as fast as possible. If I only slowed down, a Kapo or an SS-man hit me with a club on the head and on the shoulders.

Later on, it was not even necessary to murder the prisoners; they died like flies from various diseases.

Ten thousand men left the camp every morning.

Ten thousand men returned every evening from work, accompanied by a cheerful melody. But among those who returned hundreds were already dead or on the verge of dying.

Chapter 4

Roll Call Includes the Dead

In Birkenau we had to carry out various kinds of assignments, some of them hard and difficult, others easy and light. Man was treated like a motor, like a horse, like a cart. Sometimes he was just a mop, or a pick, or a rag used to scrub dirty floors.

Very often we were given silly things to do, or we had to work in a way which would make a skilled worker raise his brows. For example, when tools became scarce, one was told to gather mud and snow with bare hands and to carry it in the folds of his coat to a certain spot.

Often we had to transport a load of bricks to a marked point, and then bring them back again to the place where we found them. Some prisoners had to gather only short pieces of straw on the main road which ran through the settlement. I knew others who had been ordered to sweep floors with toothbrushes.

There was no way of fooling the guards. Each task had to be done speedily and efficiently. Many slave workers had been killed by so-called "light work."

And every day 10,000 men were registered on their way to the labor camp, and ten thousand on their way back. Corpses were listed at roll call as still living.

The Roll Calls

Roll calls took place in the morning, in the evening and occasionally at noon.

Everybody was waiting in the square. Healthy men stood in rows. The sick and the dead were laid on the ground, one next to another. Weather conditions did not change the routine. If it was a rainy day or if a snowstorm was raging, the sick would be placed in the mud near the wall.

At times, more than 100 dying men waited their turn for hours, though they did not care much whether their names were called by the guards. They thought only of another, more important roll call with God.

Those who felt strong enough to move tried to find a sheltered place or to get out of the mud, but a blokowy or izbowy (guards assigned to the barracks or to the quarters) quickly brought them to their senses by a heavy blow or by a kick in the belly.

I remember the roll call on the first day of my working assignment.

The dead and the sick had just been unloaded from the sledges and placed on the ground at the wall. The temperature had dropped to 14 degrees below zero, but in spite of the cold the ailing men had to lie for another two hours. Nevertheless some of them pulled through and remained alive.

The busiest person during roll call was the guard of each block. His task was to teach the prisoners how to stand in line. The heavy handle of a pick or an ax was a mighty weapon in the hands of a blokowy. With this tool he could shape the column and make it look perfect.

One of the less pleasant recollections is that of the morning roll call. We had no time to dress nor to swallow the cup of tepid coffee.

The shrill whistle caused a stampede of frightened men. We would run to the doors like madmen, trying to avoid the blows lavishly administered by the guard. Many latecomers appeared in the yard in bare feet and with bleeding heads and broken hands.

The slightest misdemeanor, stepping out of the row, for example, was punished with severe blows. Guards liked to use their sticks when straightening the line of prisoners.

Even now, seeing a policeman with a club makes me feel sick.

The Stubenfuehrers and Their Accomplices

In Birkenau, as in other camps, prisoners formed two distinct groups. In the nameless crowd there were always some ruthless men with depraved hearts.

It should be remembered that in concentration camps innocent men and women, political prisoners, were forced to live together with notorious murderers, ex-convicts, often vicious and degenerate men. The Germans placed them among good people on purpose, hoping that their presence would speed up the doom of the intellectuals of invaded countries.

"They will exterminate themselves with their own hands", said one of the SS-men. "That makes our work so much easier."

Camp leaders carefully selected the worst thugs and degenerate murderers and entrusted them with responsible tasks. These men became the real masters of each block. The block supervisor, or blokowy, had the right to choose his own aids: a secretary, and guardians for every dormitory, the so-called izhowi (Izba — a room).

The boss of the barracks and his aids were our dictators and tyrants. Not only could they inflict punishments, but they were also allowed to execute the "difficult ones".

Those "dictators" represented various nationalities: German, Austrian, Polish, Czech, Ukrainian and others.

The working squads had another type of boss, namely the KAPO and their aids.

A Kapo or a Blokowy whose record showed several executions gained the respect and the appreciation of SS-men. The reverse is equally true.

If a Kapo lost any interest in murdering defenseless prisoners, or became altogether fed up with his job, he quickly lost their consideration. Such a "sissy" ended his life as a common prisoner, whose condition was even worse than that of others, because he was shadowed by his former comrades.

There is nothing surprising in the fact that Kapos and their like did their utmost to prove their ruthlessness. One man with the nickname of Redhead was not satisfied with executions carried out during the day, he also visited the barracks after midnight and killed his victims.

He paid visits to our block No. 21 several times. Usually he was drunk. I remember one of his nocturnal inspections. He approached a bunk and dragged "his man to the floor, and then began to kick him around, and to club him with a stick covered with nails. The helpless victim gasped and moaned but did not die quickly enough. Exasperated, the guard finished the job by strangling the man, and then he went to another section.

I also remember two terrible killers; one of them called Januszand his friend Michael, who assassinated a great number of prisoners. Janusz was quite cynical about it.

He once said with a candid smile: "I have a young wife and two kids. See. They wait for me. I want to be able to return home. If I am a sissy with you people, I will never see them again. That's why I have to kill you. If you would know my wife and kids, you would not be surprised. Ah! They are so sweet..."

This man was a Pole. However he never saw his "sweet" wife again.

In 1943 all the guards were strangled by prisoners of Number 21. Janusz was murdered when the truck transporting prisoners to Mauthausen drove through a dark forest.

In block No. 16 we had another kind of tormentor, a German guard. He loved to stare at his victims writhing in pools of blood. Clubs and sticks he left to others. His method was different. He liked to use his bare hands, and to strangle his victims slowly but relentlessly. Very often he would hit a man and, when he collapsed on the floor, he would trample him with his heavy boots, and finally jumped with both feet on his neck, crushing the collarbone.

One winter evening after the roll call a group of guards entered block No. 16, dragging several dead men.

The bodies were stiff, the faces had a bluish hue. "Frozen to death", someone whispered. The guards placed them in a heap in a corner of the shed, where each block had its "cozy nook" in which corpses were left until morning.

Later in the night one of the victims regained consciousness and tried to crawl to the nearest bunk. The guard of the block woke up promptly, pounced on the man and began to strangle him.

"What! you've decided to live? You swine!" he shouted wildly.

"Oh, no. You've been already listed as dead. Back you go!" The dying man was thrown again on the heap of bodies, but for hours we heard stifled moans and gasps which made us shudder.

Chapter 5

"Those who live by the sword will perish by the sword."

One of the guards, the boss of block No. 16, was later hanged in Oswiecim by his German colleagues, the SS-men, because they found in his locker two large suitcases filled with gold coins, and with gold teeth, which he had extracted himself.

Gold plates and fillings brought ill luck to their owners. Not only SS-men, but also guards and Kapos were greedy collectors of precious metals.

These few examples show that man is a complex creature.

He can with God's help become a saint, but, if he follows his nature twisted by original sin, he may easily become a devil.

Degradation

While all concentration camps were based upon one common principle — the speedy extermination of conquered nations, particularly Poles and Jews — different camps specialized in different methods.

In Mauthausen and in Gusen prisoners were killed by overexertion. They had to work in deep quarries, carrying heavy blocks. They had to climb at least 100 slippery steps carved in the rock. Many prisoners lost control and fell with their load, injuring themselves and others whom they pushed into the pit.

In other camps the terrific speed of the work proved enough to destroy the toughest men.

In Sachsenhausen everything was done "on the double", even food had to be swallowed hastily and you never saw a marching column. From dawn until nightfall it was a crazy racing of frightened, haggard men.

Food was scarce in all camps, but in some of them hunger became a torture.

In Dachau, during the period from 1940 to 1943, hunger-dropsy made all prisoners look strikingly fat, with swollen baby faces. Rotten potatoes and turnips mashed in water are indeed a poor diet. Men who remembered better days, and were once fussy about their food, now would fight for some potato peels, weeds and snails.

I saw men who ate earthworms. They behaved like gourmets. Very carefully they squeezed out of the worm all the dirt and swallowed them like spaghetti.

A rare delicacy was a field mouse, a frog or a mole. Later we learned how to make them tastier. Salt and vinegar could be obtained in the camp's cantine and a field mouse soaked in vinegar and well salted tasted wonderfully good.

In spring of 1942, several prisoners broke into the laboratory of the hospital and carried away brains, which had just been removed from skulls and set aside for students of anatomy. After succeeding in hiding the brains for a while, the men had their first square meal in camp.

Even former statesmen and bankers, once well-to-do people, were only too happy to get the most coveted job of a sanitation worker. It was indeed a privilege and unusually good luck to get such a position in Dachau. Those who swept the camp roads and carried the rubbish away were envied by everyone. The street sweeper in Dachau was an aristocrat, a big shot. He could find such treasures as a rotten potato, or a cabbage leaf.

The Dachau camp was the cleanest spot in the German Reich.

As a matter of fact, it was so clean that many prisoners paid for it with their own lives. In order to maintain the dormitories in perfect condition, we often had to spend long hours in the open, even on rainy days. One could enter a dormitory only in bare feet or in socks.

Another way of speeding up the process of human extermination was that of a ruthless discipline. Corporal punishment was inflicted for the slightest infringement of prison rules. An untidy cot, a drawer which needed scrubbing, would arouse the wrath of the bosses, and you would be taught with clubs and sticks how to keep order.

Oswiecim became famous for its mass executions by firing squads. Birkenau was famous for its filth and its gas chambers.

In Birkenau there were no showers, no one had to wash in the morning. For a total of 14,000 prisoners there was not a single washbasin. The communal bath was inoperative in winter because of frozen pipes, in summer because of lack of water. In the entire camp one could get water only in two places: the toilet and a pump near the kitchen. But we had no utensils and the toilet was occupied most of the time. It was risky to approach the pump where cooks and guards could notice an intruder. And after all, eventually one would become tired of the futile strife for water.

"What's the use, anyway", the old timers would say. "You'll get dirty during the work. Forget it. That's all."

And we tried to forget such luxuries as washbasins and soap.

For more than two months only twice did I have the opportunity to wash myself thoroughly. And I was lucky.

We were assigned to a field where a ditch filled with water, a gift sent by Heaven on a rainy day, became a tub for a few of us.

The guard was lost in an animated conversation with his colleague. They were standing under a tree and could not see the bathers. Oh, how quickly one can disrobe, jump into a ditch, splash for a while in cold lovely water and get out of it, if he is prompted by two equally strong desires: to get rid of clammy and smelly dirt and to avoid attracting attention of a man with a club.

Those who insisted on shaving had to use dishwater or water from muddy puddles.

Prisoners in Birkenau were not a pretty crowd. Their dirt-covered faces took on the color of decaying flesh. Necks and hands looked even darker.

It was a picture drawn with black and grey crayon. The spectral shapes fitted well into the background of smoky clouds overhanging the crematories and fences of barbed wire charged with electricity.

Miserable rags caught by the wiring fluttered in the wind like ugly bats. They reminded us of all those who, in despair, had thrown themselves on the net charged with a deadly current.

Everything was colorless in Birkenau: the walls, covered with a drab grey paint, were soiled with blood and with human excrements.

Birds seemed to avoid the dismal place. A lonely crow or a raven was greeted as a messenger from another world.

I had a great craving for the sun, but in Birkenau even on sunny days the golden sphere was covered with clouds of smoke. It was a dead sun. Dead like the world. Dead like every one of us.

I love birds, but in Birkenau the cheerful twittering of a lark somewhere in the skies made me feel more despondent than ever. It got on my nerves. The little bird, so gay and carefree, seemed to mock me. Sometimes a bird's song sounded like a funeral dirge.

I will never forget the faces of my friends in Birkenau. They were livid and swollen. Their eyes were bloodshot, and many prisoners had sore eyelids. They had lost their eyelashes and in the morning they could not open the eyes filled with pus.

Only a painter like Goya could have caught the expressions of those tragic faces, and those twisted and crippled hands covered with scars and with blisters, hands once shapely and well kept, sensitive hands of artists, fine hands of skilled craftsmen, gentle hands of priests that had held the Sacred Host.

Gradually, our bodies got used to dirty rags, which had clothed other victims no longer alive.

In Birkenau no one could change his shirt, even if it was falling to pieces. On arrival, each prisoner was given one shirt and it had to serve him until his death, or until his transfer to another camp. These shirts became breeding ground for various vermin.

Before going to sleep, I used to organize a hunting party. Only "big game" deserved our efforts. It was not worthwhile to catch the small fry. After having crushed twenty or thirty big lice my fingernails streamed with blood. But the small fry were also a nuisance. They would bite like mosquitoes. Lazier than mosquitoes, they liked to drain one single spot, for example my chest. After several nights, I developed a large sore which was not only painful, but itched dread-fully because another ally of the lice and of German guards took hold of me: the dreaded mange.

The only way of getting rid of these pests was disinfection. In our camp, however, disinfection was applied without a previous bath and during the procedure many prisoners lost their clothes irretrievably. We went to work so exhausted because of sleepless nights that we literally dragged our feet.

"It is not worth-while to get disinfected," said the old timers, "even if we would destroy ALL the lice, others that remained in the cot would greet us during the night."

Today, as a free creature of God I am still haunted by the memory of those nights, and my clean white sheet brings me back a dim picture of my old dirty cot covered with lice.

We slept in bunks, placed one above another. One could not sit upright without bumping one's head. The wooden planks were covered with a filthy blanket. Intended for four people, the beds had ten or more occupants. No one could sleep; we gasped for lack of air.

The bunk was the only place where one could hide something: a slice of stale bread or a pair of torn slippers. For fear of being robbed of their most cherished possessions, prisoners rarely disrobed. They crawled into beds in their damp clothes, and in boots covered with a crust of mud. They were forbidden to sleep in boots, but as soon as they took them off, they did not find them in the morning.

On days free from work, we had no place to move in the "block", and we had to lie down in our wet clammy garments, which made us shiver from cold. In the narrow passage between the bunks, several barrels served as toilets.

Even in winter the dormitory did not need heating. The air was heavy with a foul smell. Many prisoners suffered from asthma and heart attacks.

Some of the barracks in Birkenau reminded me of an ancient cemetery in the caves of the Camaldolese Monastery near Cracow. As a child, I once visited those cellars where hundreds of monks had been buried in narrow graves made in the rock. The bodies of the holy men slowly disintegrated into ashes and after many years these ashes were gathered and buried in a common tomb, so that there would be place for newcomers.

In Birkenau, before the morning call, we had to remove corpses from bunks and cart them to the crematory. A new prisoner would promptly take over the cot which still bore the imprint of a human body.

Typhoid Fever

From the very beginning, typhoid fever and diarrhea were rampant in Birkenau. All sorts of germs flourished in the filthy camp, since hygienic facilities did not exist. Each prisoner had attacks of typhus and diarrhea.

There was no medical service and no first aid stations.

Those stricken with contagious diseases endeavored to carry on their daily work until a complete breakdown occurred.

Every day several men suffered from dizzy spells. Some died on the road. Others dragged on until the next day, and at dawn we had to remove their corpses from the bunks.

I had an old friend in Birkenau. His name was Lizurej. We spent several months together in the prison of Sieradz. I vividly remember his last day. He returned from work but did not have enough strength left to climb into his bunk. Suddenly he staggered and collapsed in the narrow passage. I tried to lift him, but he went into a coma and died a few hours later.

Another good friend of mine, Father Gorajecki, the vicar of Dobrzec, near Kalisz, did his utmost to finish his work only to fall without warning to the ground, overcome by the deadly disease.

I saw scores of prisoners killed by typhoid fever. We grew so used to death that we walked among corpses, like among weeds.

A widely known author who escaped from a horror camp said to me: "All those who were rescued from death camps will never forget the dreadful past. They will never become completely readjusted to normal life."

He was right.

Chapter 6

Although we escaped from hell, our hearts are broken

Hundreds of liberated men and women enjoyed the blessings of freedom for only a short while. By now they are dead.

It seems that those dreadful camps are still sending forth some kind of evil vibrations.

Gravedigger No. 2

Besides typhoid fever, another disease was the curse of Birkenau. We called it Durchfal. It had all the symptoms of diarrhea with a bloody discharge.

Out of a total of 14,000 prisoners, about 200 died every day from Durchfal. Thousands of stricken men would not eat anything, and as their rations were not cut, other prisoners could use them. Thanks to epidemics there was more food than ever before. Gradually hunger disappeared altogether. We received extra rations of bread and soup, but both soup and vegetables were actually a poison, deliberately prepared in such a way as to bring about certain ill effects.

The kitchen was supervised by SS-men, who considered it their sacred duty to help their Fuehrer in exterminating undesirable elements. When a kettle with soup or with a substitute for coffee was ready, an SS-man would order the cook to mix in it a pound of raw flour or mashed turnips unfit for consumption. Only then the kettles were sent to our blocks for distribution.

Our meals were always cold and we had to eat carefully, swallowing only cooked particles of turnips and spitting out the raw ones.

Food was distributed in the blocks, in the yard and on the field. We had to gather the improvised utensils at random and in a hurry, such as broken dishes, old pots and pans covered with rust.

In our block No. 16 unpeeled potatoes were thrown into the soup, together with mud, dung and straw. Potatoes were never washed before cooking. We ate our meals in a rush as others waited in turn. Having no spoons we used fingers. No one had strength enough to wash the dishes. We just threw them away on a heap.

No one in such conditions could enjoy good digestion.

Some of us had the dreaded durchfal several times. I was cautious. I would rather fast than eat rotten food, but in spite of all precautions during two months I had durchfal three times.

The few toilets were always besieged by ailing men.

Very often when we were driven to the labor camp a prisoner dazed with fever, suffering from a painful cramp, soiled himself and would be ruthlessly punished by inhuman guards. It was a pitiful sight to watch those sick men, either crawl to work or stay behind overcome by fever. Others tried to walk in spite of diarrhea.

During the night in the overcrowded barracks the barrels which served as toilets quickly filled up. The stench was unbearable. Men fought their way to the barrel. Others, too weak, stayed in their bunk in their own filth.

I would rather omit these repulsive details, but they give you an idea of our life in Birkenau.

At night the dead were loaded on a truck and sent to a crematory. Prisoners from various blocks assigned to these duties had to take turns. When my turn came, a group of fifty men had to carry the corpses from the shed to a truck which waited at a distance of about thirty yards. Two men grasped the stiff arms. Two others took hold of the legs. We were already exhausted after several hours of hard labor, and the load seemed heavier than a mountain, so that we simply dragged the dead on the uneven ground.

The bodies were either naked, or covered with torn remnants of a shirt, or wound dressings. It was dreadful to touch the cold, clammy flesh, often covered with horrible scars. Sometimes the body was already in a state of decomposition and parts of the skin stuck to our hands.

We worked for hours in the dark night.

When we returned to our block we had only one thought: to wash our sticky, bloody hands. Someone asked the guard to give us water. He was dismissed with curses and sneers. We tried to get rid of the dirt by rubbing our hands against our prison coats, but the odor of decaying flesh would haunt us for hours. It was suppertime. After all, one had to eat. Reluctantly we ate our bread, swallowing millions of germs and viruses.

Deprived of any kind of remedy, every prisoner finally worked out his own system of hygiene. One of my friends found that charcoal was good for stomach disorders. From that time on he always burned his piece of bread and he swallowed the black powder. Others ate charcoal from burned wood. We would recognize them by their black mouths covered with soot.

Dreams of Water

Hunger is bad enough, but there is something worse than hunger — thirst.

A man who suffers from fever will give anything for a cup of cold water. But there was no cold water in Birkenau.

In winter we discovered that snow can become a life saver. We indulged in swallowing huge pieces of frozen snow, we loved to eat icicles. How good they tasted!

In spring we looked for snow, like gold-diggers in search of a vein of gold. One had to remove heaps of rubbish in order to get to the frozen earth, and to find some thawing dirty snow. It tasted better than ice cream.

We also discovered that water in ditches was a germ carrier. It caused violent cramps and diarrhea. Only a few lucky and privileged prisoners could get boiled water or a cup of coffee. Many sick men gave up their shirts and their shoes for one cup of water.

When I was stricken with typhoid fever in SACHSENHAUSEN, thank God, I went into a coma for several days, but upon regaining consciousness I thought I would die from thirst. I remember that I found strength enough in my emaciated body to walk to the washroom (yes, there was a washroom in Sachsenhausen!) and to drink at least two quarts of water. I knew very well that it might kill me, but the temptation was too strong. Of course, I paid for it by falling ill for the fourth time.

During my illness, I often dreamed of cold water and how I would drink it without stopping.

In DACHAU, my neighbor suffered from dropsy and was forbidden any kind of liquids. But he could not stand the torture of thirst, and one night he went to the lavatory and brought some water in a stolen basin. I was the only person who knew that he kept a vessel full of tepid water under his blanket. He cared for it more than a gold digger would care for a pound of pure gold. And though he knew that drinking it would accelerate his death, he did not hesitate to swallow the dirty liquid with an expression of heavenly bliss. He died a few days later. As a former inmate of Birkenau, I knew how he felt.

In DACHAU, where hunger was driving us crazy, we would eat any kind of rubbish. Victims of thirst would gladly swallow a poisoned drink only to feel its refreshing dampness on their parched and swollen tongues.

Chapter 7

Our Enemy — the Elements

Winter and early spring were the most trying seasons. In Birkenau we had to work even during winter gales. We were not allowed to cover our ears or to put up our collars. If one was lucky enough to own a woolen rag, he would have to conceal it under his shirt.

We had no gloves, but we later learned how to protect our hands. The ingenuity of prisoners was amazing. Small bags shaped like gloves were made from rags. Other men used all the paper available near the cement works. It proved an excellent wrapping for the feet. We placed sheets of dirty paper on our chests and stomachs. Without those paper shields I would have certainly frozen to death.

We also learned another lesson: when your legs and hands become numb and stiff, the best way of avoiding chillblains is to move the limbs continuously. We did not have enough energy to warm our hands by blowing on them, so we had to resort to some kind of exercise. However, during a snowstorm we were helpless. There was nothing else to be done except to hide in a ditch or stay close to one another. The worst experience was a gale with snow and rain which thoroughly drenched our miserable prison garb and made us shiver under the icy shower.

Birkenau was set up on marshes; spring melted all the snow leaving a treacherous swampland. Only the main road was paved with stones. Other roads and yards seemed to dissolve and drag us into a muddy trap. Even though one had boots or a strong pair of shoes, they would soon be drenched and heavy with splashing water.

Most of the prisoners had only old slippers which got lost in the mud and could not be recovered; and then they had to walk back to the camp barefoot. The real victims, however, were the sick. They had to lie in the mud for hours. Several men literally drowned in it and choked to death.

Nervous breakdowns and suicides never occurred more often than during that gloomy hopeless season. I was often awakened by wild shooting. I learned later that some prisoners, who had reached the end of their rope, just walked out and begged the SS-men who stood on their watchtowers to kill them. This request would always be graciously and cheerfully fulfilled. SS-men delighted in carrying out any kind of executions.

Hitler had established a special decoration, called WARSCHAU-SCHIELD (the Warsaw shield), for

German soldiers who distinguished themselves during the siege of Warsaw in 1939. In a concentration camp the shooting of a prisoner was rewarded by a vacation. "If you wish to spend a weekend with your cutie, — kill a KACET", that was the slogan of all guards. Each victim was then listed on a board and the total of executed men determined the number of free hours awarded the executioner.

On the Russian Front four generals won the final battle: FROST, SNOW, MUD and RAIN. In concentration camps, the same elements caused the death of thousands of prisoners.

Every morning, after roll call, we were ordered to remove from the barbed wire the bodies of those who had ended their lives. Some of them were still breathing. Strangely enough, there was never an epidemic of suicides in any of these concentration camps. It seems rather puzzling, but the truth is that Christian faith became the source of infinite patience and fortitude. The others who had no faith still carried some hope and believed that tomorrow would be better. No one, I believe, thought that Germany would, in the long run, win the war.

When Death Came

In the Sieradz prison, I was shocked when I saw the guards stripping the bodies of the dead of their rags and throwing them in a wooden box with a piece of paper instead of a shroud. These "caskets" were carted away by Polish nuns who had to bury them in the local cemetery.

In German concentration camps, such as Birkenau, that would seem a luxury. There were no caskets and no paper shrouds.

After the morning roll call a group of prisoners was assigned to the task of removing the dead from dormitories. They were dragged to a shed connected with barrack No. 23. Sometimes a body was carelessly thrown across a wheelbarrow with its arms and legs sweeping the ground; sometimes it was carried on a plank or on stretchers made of two sticks. Often, a prisoner had to carry a corpse on his back, and if the load was too heavy, he threw it on the ground and dragged it in the mud.

Once, two young prisoners approached me and one of them said: "Father, have you ever followed this kind of funeral? Do you remember what a fuss we made over our dear dead? How we dressed them! How we mourned them! How we tried to make them look impressive in their last garb, in a glow of lights, and amidst costly wreaths with golden inscription on silky ribbons! Here at least our relatives will not have any trouble with our remains. We have been treated like dogs, and like dogs we will be buried."

"Do you think, Father, that there is a God in Heaven?" asked others, who felt their faith shaken and vainly tried to find an answer to their doubts.

I would not censure these unfortunate men, who for the first time in their lives were facing seemingly insolvable problems.

At nightfall, another sort of funeral procession took place between the sheds filled with corpses and the crematories, where a big fire would turn all bodies into a pile of ashes. Later on, relatives would receive a short message and a small package with several ounces of dark grey powder. But even a bereaved mother would not attach much importance to this "relic". No one was sure whether the ashes were really the remains of the victim.

A skeptical person brought to a Polish laboratory a few ounces of dark powder without saying what it was. The man in charge of the laboratory, after analyzing it, found that the ashes were remnants of burnt weeds and rags.

"Medical Care"

Most of the camps had an infirmary. It was situated at a certain distance in an enclosure. Soon, very soon, prisoners lost any delusions abut its efficiency. We called the infirmary a finishing chamber (Wykonczalnia).

At first, no medical help was ever offered, and the sick were simply left in the infirmary, where they would die from illness or else be finally disposed of in a gas chamber.

The Germans found out several methods of "finishing" the sick. A friend of mine, Mr. Niziuk, told me about his personal experiences in one of these finishing hospitals.

Each day an SS-officer would make the round of the ward. He had pleasant manners and a charming smile. Like an angel sent by Heaven, he greeted all the sick and approached each bed, bestowing kind words and genuine sympathy. Chatting with those able to talk, he inquired like a friend about their health, asked them if they were married, how many children were waiting for "daddy" at home, and so on, and so on. He made some notes in a small pocketbook.

After his visit, another officer would come and read a list of names. Those listed were ordered to disrobe, to leave their shirts and to go to the operating hall. No one returned from such a trip. The operation was a simple one. One injection of quicksilver. Death came instantly.

Sometimes the SS-man was too busy to talk. He stood for a while in the middle of the room and sought out his victims by merely looking at the patients.

From my own experience, I know the DACHAU methods very well.

Once in a while, all the sick were told that they would be transferred to a sanatorium. This sounded attractive, and of course many prisoners volunteered to register. They were promptly and graciously granted a pass to the nursing home. While storing the garments, which were sent back to camp after the departure of patients, we found small slips of paper covered with hastily scribbled messages: "We have been betrayed. We are doomed. Don't get registered. It was a trap."

After this discovery, no one asked to be sent to a convalescent home. Selected victims had to be forcibly removed. From DACHAU, 112 patients and 277 Polish Catholic priests were sent to gas chambers near Linz.

The camps had several special trucks equipped with "gas chambers". In these unusual limousines, prisoners could be easily executed on their way to a crematory.

As late as 1944, two thousand sick men unable to work had been sent from DACHAU to MAJDANEK near LUBLIN, where a deliberately ruthless treatment caused the death of uncounted victims.

In many instances, guards selected by SS-men liquidated the sick on the spot, thus helping the Reich to speed up the process of mass extermination of vanquished peoples. A guard who efficiently carried out his bloody assignment got more and better food or a lighter job.

A sick man who soiled his bunk was dragged to a washroom, where so-called "male nurses" poured a stream of cold water on his head until he died. If he refused to die quickly, they forced in his mouth a rubber pipe and made him choke to death.

These male nurses delighted in kicking and clubbing their helpless victims. They deprived them of their meager rations, and the only obituary we heard sounded as follows: "Fine! I'll get his ration". They helped SS-men in administering injections of various poisons or forced the sick to swallow lethal pills.

I doubt whether any of the horror camps had a more gruesome infirmary than Birkenau. Here the treatment was harsh and inexorable.

Very often at nightfall, all barracks crammed with men would be locked up and no one could get out. We all knew that another storm was approaching. During the searches (szpeia), all sorts of diabolic schemes invented by degenerate SS-men would be carried out, —mass executions, corporal punishment, frightening searching parties.

I remember vividly one of these performances (and it was the first time I witnessed one). We suddenly heard the deafening noise of motors. In the courtyard, searchlights began to sweep the blocks. I did not know what it meant. But at dawn, during roll call, I saw numerous signs of a fire in the yard. I asked one of the prisoners what had happened. The old timer grinned at me and whispered: "The entire infirmary has been dispatched to hell".

The next day we learned the truth. (Somehow truth always found its way in to the concentration camps.) All the inmates of the infirmary were sent to the gas chamber. Not too many victims, just 1,180.

A few reckless men had succeeded in finding hideouts, where they would stay unnoticed for a day or two. Others crawled under heaps of dead bodies, wishing that they could stay there forever. But in the long run, no one would be able to escape.

This kind of house cleaning occurred in at least twice a month.

Usually more than 1,000 men landed in gas chambers, and though the work was done stealthily during the night it never passed unnoticed. We had a wonderful news service which never failed. Gradually it became more and more difficult for SS-men to lure us into the "sanatorium" trap. We would rather die in the fields or in a filthy dormitory under the blows of a supervisor, than choke to death under an invisible shower. Only those numbed by fever were easily transferred to the "sanatoriums".

In many German camps, men in excellent physical condition were used for medical experiments. They became guinea pigs for new serums and drugs, used against malaria and inflammatory tumors caused by malnutrition. Prisoners who developed phlegmatical boils had dreadful gangrenous wounds. Parts of their body literally disintegrated, showing open wounds with protruding bones.

BIRKENAU had several research laboratories in the immediate neighborhood of the gas chambers. I heard from trustworthy friends of mine, former prisoners, about various tests which killed thousands of young, sturdy men and women. It is also true that human skin was used by Germans for the manufacture of pocketbooks and of lampshades and other gruesome souvenirs. These horrid exhibits found in DACHAU proved more convincing than long reports printed on ordinary paper.

Prisoners with interesting tattoos on their bodies were kept on a special diet. When they gained weight and their skin became smooth, they received a lethal dose of some poisonous drug and were sent to a workshop, where expert skinners would prepare the tattooed parts for further use.

Men with an unusual shape of the cranium were also disposed of and their heads were preserved in the anatomical museum. Handsome young men and girls with a perfect bone structure had to die because nice skeletons were sought by German universities.

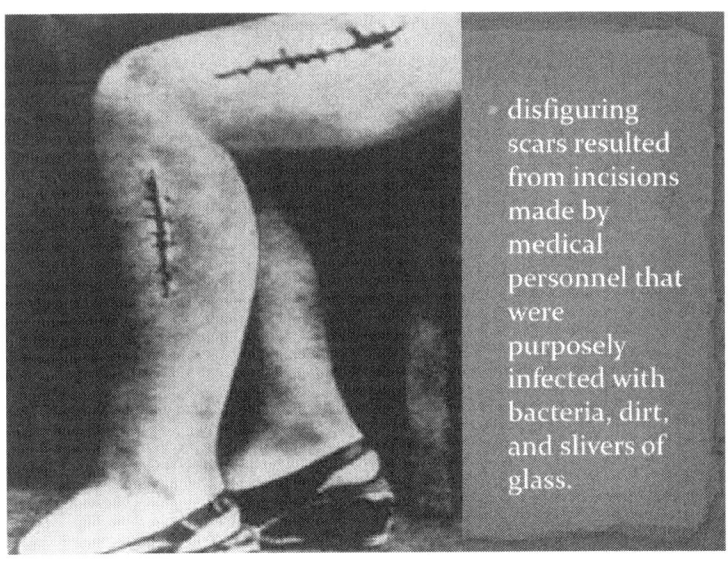

disfiguring scars resulted from incisions made by medical personnel that were purposely infected with bacteria, dirt, and slivers of glass.

Chapter 8

"Burn the Rubbish"

Each camp had its own methods.

IN DACHAU the sick were sent "somewhere".

IN SACHSENHAUSEN they died from exertion and malnutrition.

In BIRKENAU they were asphyxiated.

At dawn, all prisoners including the invalids had to rush into the courtyard for the morning call. Before assigning them to work in a quarry or in the fields, supervisors made a thorough inspection of all "candidates". If they saw a haggard and drowsy man, they would order him to quit. A working team had to be composed of able bodied and tough fellows not of decrepit weaklings; and besides, everyone in the camp got tired of dragging back those who died from over-exertion or who collapsed in a deep quarry. It caused delays for which a camp supervisor was responsible.

After the departure of the working squad, the camps were still crammed with men, mostly hospital cases, emaciated and half conscious. It was forbidden to stay in the dormitories and they had to hide in dark nooks, in closets, behind heaps of rubbish. Many stayed for hours in the latrines. These were overcrowded and one could die there from lack of air, but they were a fairly cozy place to wait in unnoticed by guards, while the labor battalion returned.

Once or twice a week, about midday, a caravan of empty lorries would stop in the courtyard. SS-men and camp guards rounded up all hopeless cases. It was a regular manhunt in the labyrinth of dormitories and hideouts. All the sick were forced into the trucks. With a typically German love for order, the SS-men requisitioned all the caps and hats and gave the signal for departure. The mysterious caravan started on its journey to the accompaniment of curses and screams. We knew that the journey's end would be in a dark forest at the gates of a gas chamber.

When an animal can run, it still has a chance to escape, but when it has been hit in the legs, it can only crawl and wait for death. That was how I felt in Birkenau. A prisoner who could not walk was lost. He had no chance of escaping. Lame or shaky limbs were an ominous sign of approaching doom.

The Outcasts

In Chicago, where I now live, as I look out through my window I often see a policeman helping children cross Colfax street. He is a big fellow with a calm, pleasant face. Children love him. They gladly grasp his hand and try to take as long paces as he does.

Whenever I see this familiar scene I feel good.

"Here is a country", I say to myself, "where kindness is not judged as a sign of weakness, a country where a little child is treated with respect."

And again memories of Dachau and of Birkenau rise from the past like dark, heavy clouds. In those awful places of confinement man was crushed like a little insect.

If I were to attempt to depict the tragedy of the Jews in German prisons, I would need the gift of a great writer. I will, however, give a few examples and you may draw your own conclusions.

While waiting in prison for a final verdict, I met many Jews. Their mass extermination was only started. In 1943 an order issued by German authorities in Berlin became the signal for an unending pilgrimage of prisoners to concentration camps. All prisoners who received long-term sentences were sent to camps. The order contained a short addition: "ALL Jews, even those who have no sentences, should be transferred to concentration camps".

At first one would meet thousands of Jews in each camp, but eventually a Jew was seldom seen in any place of confinement. In Sachsenhausen in 1943 there were only 80 Jews, skilled watchmakers who were retained to repair watches of SS-men and other German officials. In Dachau no Jews were left, aside from several Germans of Jewish origin. Some of them had served in the German army. They had distinguished themselves and had many decorations and medals. (These, of course, had been confiscated by camp supervisors.) When the truth about their descent came out, they were promptly sent to concentration camps.

The largest number of Jews was kept in the infamous OSWIECIM (Auschwitz) prison. BIRKENAU, a branch of Oswiecim, was indeed a "motherhouse" of all Jews. Out of a total of 14,000 prisoners, 7,000 Jews lived in special blocks. Some Jews became high-ranking officials in the camp administration. Through what devious ways they achieved such a distinction remains their personal secret.

One could easily recognize a Jew. Nobody looked more forlorn and ragged.

In winter they shivered in their light coats. Their overalls were filthy, their faces covered with blistering wounds.

High-strung and emotional, they often quarreled among themselves, fighting wildly for a piece of bread or because of some trifling offense. Driven to work with whips, forced to perform abominable and degrading tasks, pushed and abused by sadistic SS-men, they died like flies.

It is a sad truth that Jews did not get much help even from their fellow sufferers. I myself saw prisoners stripping an old Jew of his shirt. They had a hard time to hide a slice of stale bread.

Once during work I saw a Jewish youngster. He was probably 14 years old. Shivering in his flimsy overalls, he leaned on his spade and cried bitterly.

He had an intelligent, sensitive face and very fine hands. He gave the impression of a well educated boy from a wealthy family. Other prisoners had robbed him of his last glove. After several hours of hard labor on a bitterly cold day, his hands were red and stiff. Exhausted and downhearted, he could hardly move.

I tried to cheer him up: "My dear boy, try to swing your arms, up and down, back and forth. Otherwise you will freeze to death. You are young. You will get out of this hell." The boy looked at me wistfully and broke again in tears.

"Father, do not waste your time", another prisoner, a student from Poznan, whispered in my ear. "The boy is doomed. He will be sent tomorrow to the gas chamber. I heard the camp guard read his name."

Gradually conditions in the concentration camps became so appalling that even SS-men shunned our blocks, for fear of contracting some contagious disease. But even the fear of contagion would not prevent German Jew baiters from entering their dormitories in order to torture a helpless prisoner.

From afar we often could see an SS-man who liked to invent all sorts of diabolic tricks to prolong the martyrdom of his victim. He would lash and club him, he would order him to dance in the snow, to make somersaults and finally to jump on the high wired fence, charged with electricity.

Whenever an SS-man visited our block, he ordered the shoemakers to prepare new rawhide whips, and he never failed to add: "That's for those d...Jews!"

I was once sent to the grounds of a projected crematory, and I saw an SS-man forcing an aged Jew to jump into a hole in the frozen pond. He then stood for a while on the shore and roared with laughter, while the drowning man desperately endeavored to keep his head above the water. He finally disappeared under the thick ice.

A Jewish industrialist from Berlin was one of the rare cases of immediate surrender and resignation. He knew that he would die, and he even had a premonition when he would be sent to the gas chamber. This friend of mine predicted a long time in advance the date of his "final journey" and refused to be consoled.

"I do not know how the German horror show will end," he used to say, "but I know that all Jews who are now in the camp are doomed. I rather wish to meet death with a contemptuous smile, than to wriggle and scream like others do. Our executioners are delighted when we lose our minds from fear. My only revenge is to deprive them of this pleasure."

Many Jews showed wonderful courage and fortitude, many died, like heroes and saints. A young Jewish boy from the Polish city of Lodz was overcome by typhoid fever. The same day the camp leader of our block (No. 16) beat him almost to a pulp. Streaming with blood and staggering, the young man dragged himself to the dispensary, where he found enough strength to shout at the top of his voice:

"I am going to die for my people and for my fatherland. Long live Poland. Long live the Polish and Jewish people. Brothers have courage..."

After the liberation, only a few Jews were found in German camps. If they lasted so long, it was only thanks to exceptional shrewdness. Some Jews succeeded in concealing their origin, and if they did not have the characteristic features of the Semitic race, they could somehow get lost in the crowd. Others had their own method of moving from one hideout to another. Skilled workers and experts were spared by Germans for use in factories and laboratories.

Under Hitler's regime, thousands of innocent people were continuously put to death in concentration camps set up in various parts of Germany and later in invaded countries. The German people were perfectly aware of their mass executions and of the sinister crimes committed in concentration camps, which spread in the vicinity of towns and cities, but they would rather keep quiet then expose themselves to reprisals.

Thousands of SS-men and Gestapo officials employed by the administration had numerous relatives who lived outside the prisons. Thousands of SS-men and Gestapo employees would occasionally relate some "funny stories" about their Jewish or Polish victims to make the people laugh.

Unfortunately, besides a few courageous and indomitable men, like Cardinal Faulhaber, nobody seemed to get upset at the fact that undesirable elements, such as Jews or patriots of invaded countries, were burned alive or tortured to death.

It would be of no avail to throw anathema on the guilty. It will not bring back the dead, but we must endeavor to reshape the world in a way that these mass murders may never occur again. Godless doctrines, rabid nationalism, pride and hate must be eradicated from our lives. Parties or individuals cannot be allowed to enslave human beings. Lasting peace will never be achieved, unless it is based upon Christ's Teachings and the Ten Commandments.

It sounds incredible that 3,000,000 Jews could have been eliminated in death camps, but that is the plain truth.

Birkenau — Hecatomb of the Jewish People

For two months, while working on the road and near the crematory, I witnessed mass executions of thousands of human beings. The Camp of Birkenau became indeed a Jewish graveyard.

Each day new carloads of Jews arrived at the station, where prisoners were promptly segregated. Some young and healthy men and women had to go to separate labor camps, others were forced into vans and sent to gas chambers.

Eventually, for lack of time, only ten percent of the new arrivals were chosen as working teams. Later on, entire convoys disappeared in the gas chambers immediately upon their arrival.

The routine was as follows: When a carload of Jews from Cracow, Lodz, Warsaw or some other city arrived at OSWIECIM (Auschwitz), it was sidetracked and everyone was ordered to get out and wait for trucks which would bring the prisoners to the camp.

The crowd of bewildered, haggard men and women waited in silence, until the sound of rolling trucks would stir them into motion. There was no time for idle talk. German guards bullied and intimidated the newcomers. They pushed them into the trucks — mothers together with their babies, old, bearded rabbis, well groomed young girls and youngsters. No guards were needed. No one would jump out of the speeding truck which was followed by several others.

Jews brought here from Polish cities had no illusions as to the final outcome of their journey, but they still had some hope of escaping the inevitable. Only when the caravan passed by the camp and entered a dark forest, with overhanging clouds of smoke, they knew it was the end.

Once in a while, a crowd of Jewish prisoners would burst into screams, but gradually the Jews developed a fatalistic resignation. Only a few men or women would go into fits of hysterical sobbing. Those who had succeeded in smuggling a few dollars would tear the bills to pieces; others threw from the truck valuables or heirlooms, gold wedding bands, watches, more often loose precious stones easier to conceal than heavy rings and brooches.

Jews from other European countries had more stamina and optimism. Young boys and girls would cheerfully greet our working squads. They obviously did not even guess the grim truth.

At the door of a wooden shed several SS-men and their bloodhounds waited for them.

The first roll call took place in a spacious barrack. Prisoners had to disrobe.

"We will get a shower," the people whispered.

However at least one man or a woman knew too well what kind of shower was being prepared. They would break down and scream for help. A frantic stampede to the door would follow.

The milling crowd, rounded up by armed SS-guards, would fight with them. Many SS-men lost their lives in such a melee, shot to death with their own guns grabbed by reckless prisoners. It did not happen often. The victims knew too well what their efforts would prove futile and that all rebels would be subdued and murdered.

Naked men and women were searched by SS-men who looked for diamonds, and gold in the mouths and in the thick curly hair of women. Even children were not spared the ordeal.

Eventually a gate would open and the prisoners were rushed into a public bath with showers and sinks. The ceiling was covered with a net of narrow water pipes, but instead of water, deadly gas would flow from" them with a sinister whistling.

The bath lasted ten to twelve minutes. Never longer. SS-men looked at the show through round windows. They enjoyed it tremendously. They had a wonderful time peeping at the scene.

Dante never dreamt of this kind of torture when he described the inferno. A crowd-of-men, women and children gasped and chocked from lack of air. Overcome by fumes, they trampled over those who had already collapsed. They pushed their way to the door and died near it. Corpses piled up near the exit.

A few minutes later, when the last wriggling body lay motionless on the ground covered with blood and disgorged food, guards with gas masks would open the doors and remove the remains. Some bodies were still warm and quivering. An injection of adrenaline might have been able to rekindle the flickering spark of life but that would be against the rules of the omnipotent German State: all the dead and the dying had to be thrown in the fire of a crematory.

In the meantime, another caravan of trucks would stop in front of the public bath, and the show would go on. It was indeed going on uninterruptedly for months, day and night, night and day.

When we think of hell, we have only a dim idea of the sufferings of those who voluntarily have forsaken God and chosen the way of Evil. The concentration camps were well equipped to become a replica of hell on earth. Even now, writing my diary in a quiet monastery, I feel a cold shiver creeping along my spine, whenever memory brings me back the picture of that earthly Gahanna.

If every human being would be allowed to see in a glimpse the real Hell, I suppose that no one would ever commit a mortal sin lest he might become the prey of dark forces.

But too often we close our eyes and refuse to look at spectacles which remind us of our own wretchedness.

Upon my arrival in the United States, I was bitterly disappointed that people who did not live through horrible experiences under a totalitarian regime refused to look at the pictures showing gas chambers and mountains of human ashes. I do not blame them any more. Only those who were in it and had a miraculous escape are able to look again and again on the ghastly reminder of the wretchedness of modern man.

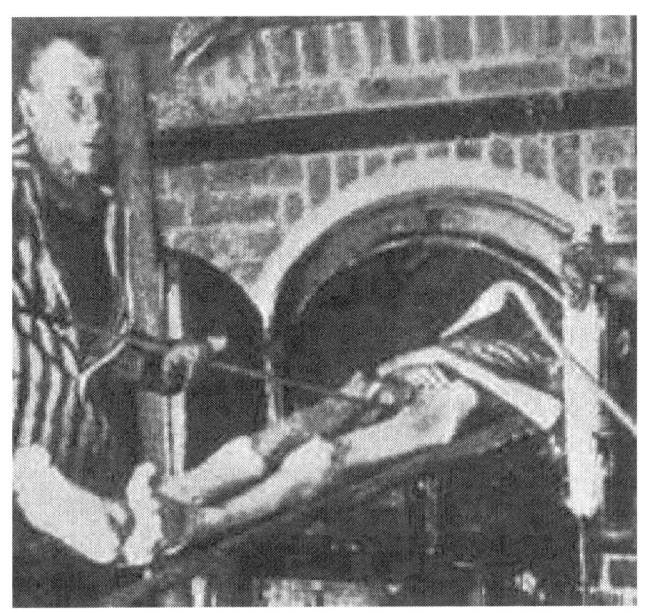

Chapter 9

The Holocaust

We all acquired certain allergies and mannerisms in the camps. For example, I hate the sight of smoking factory chimneys. Heavy smoke reminds me of millions of innocent men and women slaughtered and burned by the modern Cain whose brow has been marked with the sign of the swastika.

In 1943, at Birkenau, three crematories were active for twenty-four hours a day without interruption. I worked there as an assistant mason, and that is why I got so well acquainted with the sinister spot.

As a Catholic, I will always condemn the barbarian way of disposing of the dead in ovens. A crematory is a bad thing in itself, even if it is used for the purpose of getting rid of inanimate bodies. It is an evil heritage left by our heathen forefathers who did not believe in an immortal soul.

In Germany crematories were often used as instruments of punishment and as factors of death for mass executions.

Special crews of workers, mostly Jews and Germans, had to perform various duties in those dreadful forges. They worked in shifts. After two or three months, the entire group would be shot as undesirable witnesses. German authorities did their utmost to conceal the names and professions of their victims. They also tried to prevent the gathering of statistical data concerning the number of executions. However, news of the shocking happenings leaked out and spread all over the camp. One example consisted of the strange phenomenona that were noticed during the execution of a saintly priest in Dachau.

His body was thrown into the fire but it would not burn. Three times the guards removed it from the oven filled with ashes of other burned bodies, and finally had to bury him in the ground. Flames would not touch the remains of the holy man.

Workers assigned to the gruesome task of piling up the corpses on the stake used long iron hooks which pierced and tore the flesh. The procedure in the crematory lasted about an hour. It depended upon the degree of heat. When the fire did its work to the very end, only ashes were left on the stake and heavy smoke with particles of flesh and of coal rose from the chimneys.

Strangely enough, the smoke would sometimes change its color, from black to yellow or white.

White or golden smoke reminded me of burned incense during religious services.

We seldom knew who had been thrown into the oven, but we tried to guess what kind of a person it was. We learned to read the answer in the color of the smoke.

When the saintly Bishop KOZAL was murdered in DACHAU and his body was thrown into the "forge", all prisoners who had known him and admired his heroic behavior looked at the chimneys, trying to guess which column of smoke was once his body. When they saw a beautiful white cloud bursting from the chimney, they all had but one reaction:

"Look! That was certainly Bishop Kozal.

"Priests in our camp prayed to him as to the patron saint of all the fearful, timorous, despondent fellow sufferers who needed his powerful support.

Ashes piled up in the vicinity of the crematory would be gradually sent in small packages to relatives of the murdered men, as a last trick played by Hitler and his servants. The ashes contained particles of thousands of victims, or they were the remains of some burned rubbish. But the relatives were "regular suckers", as one guard confided; they would take anything that would remind them of their "dear ones".

In time of epidemic or of mass executions, the crematories proved too small and inadequate. Guards would not bother to clean up the ovens and to make place for newcomers. Corpses were thrown in a pile near the camp. IN DACHAU on the day of the liberation, American troops found about 2,000 corpses set aside for burning.

In Birkenau the system was different.

Crematories filled with human remains could not accommodate all the corpses. There was no time to set up new ovens. Trucks with the dead and the dying were directed to the woods.

In a clearing, stakes made of planks and rafters from abandoned buildings became funeral pyres for thousands of martyrs. Dead bodies and sometimes-living persons were "sandwiched" between several tiers of planks. Such a stake, sprayed with gasoline or with petroleum, would burn for hours, often throughout the night. In the meantime, another stake was hastily prepared for a new carload of human "fuel".

The forests and meadows looked strange and frightening behind this curtain of heavy smoke. The air was polluted, and even now it seems to me that I am swallowing the sickly smell of burned human flesh.

Our Neighbors

Men, women and gypsies had separate camps in Birkenau. Each enclosure was surrounded by a high wire fence and by a ditch filled with dirty water.

SS-men kept continuous guard on their watchtowers. Overseers and spies would be on the lookout all the time, and would sound the alarm at the slightest sign of insubordination.

When I came to Birkenau, 15,000 women lived in old stables. They were mostly Jewish, Polish and Ukranian women, but there were also numerous girls from Italy, Yugoslavia, from Greece and other countries.

It was forbidden to enter the women's enclosure. The only men who had access to them were the SS guards or skilled workers.

At nightfall a group of prisoners was often sent to the woman's camp in order to remove and cart the dead to the crematories.

"It is even worse than here", I was told by one of my friends. —

"Many corpses have smashed heads, others are decapitated. I also saw corpses with arms and legs missing. They must have been tortured in a fiendish way, these poor girls. I could not look at them.'"

One of our plumbers saw a German woman guard push a sick girl from a bunk to the floor. Another man told me that an unconscious woman with a dreadful wound in her head was lying on the bunk, unattended.

In February of 1943 I met several women in the woods where we were digging a pond. The labor squad consisted of 80 men and 200 women.

It was a hard job indeed. One had to use a heavy shovel to throw the mud on the shore where a dyke was under construction. The men worked on the dyke, the girls had to drain the pond. They trampled for hours over the swampy ground, losing their miserable footwear. Any kind of shoes, even strong walking boots, would be hopelessly worn out during such labor.

The girls returned to the camp at nightfall in their bare feet, hoping to find somewhere a pair of old slippers. More often, they would be punished for having lost their footwear.

We would see them next day, barefooted and shivering from cold, in the dark woods where even nature seemed to collaborate with our tyrants.

The women in the camp looked even more ragged than men. The majority still had their summer dresses. No one had a warm sweater or a pair of stockings. Their section had no washroom, but there were some privileged creatures who were allowed to bathe and to wash their clothes.

I met one of them. One day, all the girls toiled and sweated in the forest, while their overseer, a young and pretty Yugoslav woman, was having a good time with our guard, the dreaded Kapo. She had a nice dress, a warm coat, silk stockings and a lot of makeup on her round childish face. She also had a heavy club in her be-gloved hands.

We knew her only too well. We often saw her insulting and clubbing older women who could not work as fast as their younger colleagues. She could not bear the sight of those who suffered diarrhea. She hated to see them abandon their work and hide behind the bushes. She would attack them with her club and would shower them with dirty curses.

It fitted in the German project of mass extermination to place notorious criminals and hardboiled prostitutes together with honest people. The worst among them were chosen from prisons and from houses of ill repute in occupied countries and in Germany. When placed in concentration camps, they gladly collaborated with German authorities in corrupting and persecuting their fellow sufferers.

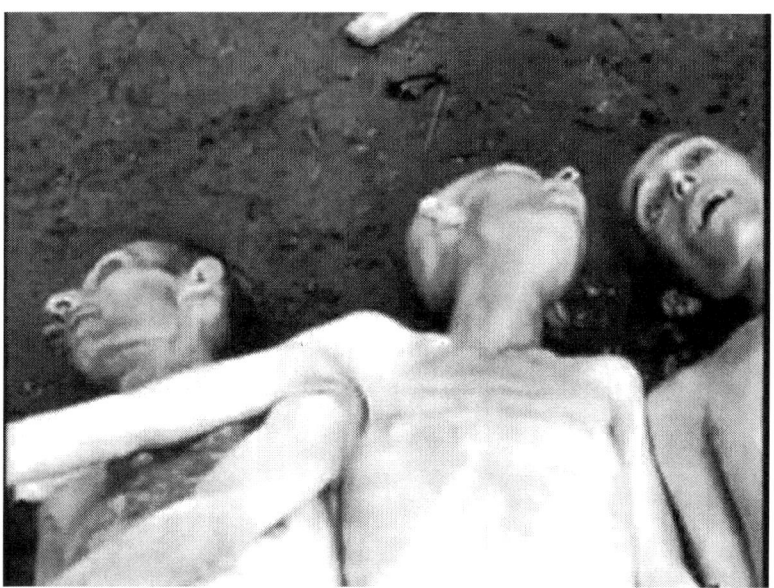

These females enjoyed various privileges. They were the only women in the camp who looked fresh and well groomed. They used lipstick and nail polish. The others had a sickly greyish complexion and glassy eyes with swollen eyelids. Their hands, often shapely and sensitive, were covered with blisters and blackened with mud.

Painted lips and scarlet nails will always remind me of those vile camp wardens, who cooperated with SS-men in crushing the resistance of captives. They will also remind me of those unfortunate small boys who became passive tools in the hands of degenerate German officials. The little boys, clad in fancy costumes, looked like weird puppets. Some of them had already acquired revolting mannerisms. They were arrogant and cynical. Others did not yet lose the charm of innocence. They were all doomed.

I often saw in nightmares feverish eyes pleading for help. I saw the pathetic robots tramping the marshland and leaving bloodstained marks. I heard the sobbing of enslaved children, and I would wake up desperately wishing a sudden and merciful death for all of us. In no other camp did the women have to endure as much as in Birkenau.

Young girls, Polish and Ukrainian students or former housewives, would approach us stealthily during the work and ask for a pair of old socks, or a dirty rag to protect their bleeding feet. We had nothing to offer, but one could not remain insensible to their bashful and pleading voices. We did our utmost to find or to steal some discarded slippers, and we brought them to the forest, sneaking every little gift with the shrewdness of old smugglers.

I never saw a more despondent looking crowd of prisoners. Sometimes they would inquire about their relatives and their friends lost in the turmoil. They seldom smiled, and they ignored the jokes made by fellow prisoners who tried to cheer them up. While in the men's camp a sense of humor was often the only weapon, captive women seemed to wither and wane like flowers deprived of light and of air.

In Birkenau there was another mysterious group of young women whom we saw only occasionally and from afar. They could be seen from time to time on the main street of the camp settlement, marching to the strains of sentimental music. Three girls led the procession. They played on banjos and mandolins. All these women had expensive gowns and a stylish hairdo. It really looked like a fashion show. These handsome and cheerful women, escorted by SS-men, were an unusual sight in the horror camp. They always entered a building which once had served as a crematory.

What was their assignment — we often wondered. I never saw them returning from such a "stroll". The puzzle seemed insolvable.

In the women's division, expectant mothers had to undergo a special kind of torture. Immediately after having given birth, the mother would be sent to work and her baby was handed over to a German camp ward. The child was strangled and thrown in a coal stove. Our work team which had to remove corpses never found any trace of infants in the dormitories, even though news of births was often brought by girls working on the dyke.

In 1943 we saw the first convoys of gypsies in Birkenau. A new settlement of barracks was built for the "gypsies' reservation". Even SS-men admired the exotic beauty of their women and their picturesque and rich costumes. They would help them in carrying their luggage and baby carriages.

The wealthy gypsies came mostly from Hungary, from Austria and Romania; the poor ones came from Eastern Poland.

Strangely enough, the gypsies who used to lead a dangerous and adventurous life showed little stamina and endurance. We often noticed in our gypsy colleagues symptoms of a complete breakdown. Many died a few weeks after their arrival. They all became an easy prey for all sorts of diseases.

Small children deprived of water and of milk died in great numbers and were followed by adults. Two or three months seemed to be the limit for an imprisoned gypsy.

Hitler wanted to destroy the Jewish race because of its wealth which he wanted for his party. The Reich would swallow and digest even gold teeth extracted from Jewish mouths. The Fuehrer was obsessed with a fear of Jews as potential carriers of communistic propaganda. Every Jew was doomed in Eastern Europe. Jewish children were also murdered as prospective communists. It proved so easy to kill a child. SS-men would grab Jewish babies by their feet and crush their heads on a wall.

Slavs became another target for Hitler's deadly weapons. He wanted to undermine this healthy and courageous race and to destroy its elite, so that he might become the undisputed ruler of Eastern Europe. He even thought of introducing compulsory sterilization of all young men. One of the preparatory steps was the devilish laboratory set up in every German camp where prisoners, men and women, were forcibly sterilized.

Gypsies were also sentenced to death. Loafers and tramps have no right to live — that was Hitler's slogan.

All the insane and neurotics treated in various German sanatoriums and in hospitals of occupied countries were eliminated "en masse'

After liquidating millions of Jews and Slavs, Hitler commenced the house cleaning among the Gypsies. Probably most of the European Gypsies, who at the time of the German invasion in 1939 roamed across Central and Eastern Europe, disappeared from the globe, crushed by the iron club of Nazism.

Chapter 10

A Tower of Babel

A German concentration camp was a conglomeration of diverse national groups. In MAJDANEK near Lublin men and women from numerous European countries were relentlessly put to death.

In DACHAU prisoners represented more than thirty-five nations. OSWIECIM (Auschwitz) and DACHAU had the largest number of Poles; in SACHSENHAUSEN and in the other death camps Russians and Ukrainians formed the bulk of inhabitants.

I noticed a surprising solidarity among the people of one race. They kept together. They had a kind of whispered news service in their own language. Ties of common tradition and of common language never proved more important than in DAYS OF CALAMITY. They were never stronger than in dungeons and in horror camps.

It would be difficult to give a clear picture of the behavior of the various national groups, since each was a motley crowd of noted scientists and of illiterates, of priests, distinguished diplomats, artists and factory workers, heroic underground insurgents and notorious burglars and gangsters.

Warm-hearted unselfish men had to share bunks with hardboiled thugs. Questionable characters and noble idealists, fearless patriots and timorous egotists, had to live side by side in the same room.

POLES as a group were probably the most ingenious in grappling with obstacles. They were stubborn and resourceful and made the most of every opportunity.

Poland had a long tradition of wars for independence. Every Polish family had at least one or two heroes, who in the past centuries fought German or Mongolian invaders, who joined the irregular armies of 1830 and of 1833, or who had to learn the mother language in secret for fear of German or of Russian oppressors.

The new calamity that befell Poland after twenty years of regained freedom gave its inhabitants a new opportunity of proving their courage and fortitude.

Prisoners of Polish origin had more stamina and optimism than others who did not have a tradition of a continuous struggle for freedom. No one in the camp was more adroit in obtaining political information, no one was more clever in finding or in remaking clothes and shoes, no one was more ingenious in providing himself and his pals with extra food or with a better job. They had a wonderful sense of humor, and it proved a powerful weapon. Thanks to this God-sent gift, they were able to live through the darkest hours. Even the worst among them had a strong faith in God, and all, good and bad —shared a strong belief in ultimate Justice. They never lost hope, and knew what would be the final outcome of the German "Drang nach Osten".

One could, recognize a Pole by the label with a capital "P" attached to his clothes, which looked surprisingly clean and in good condition. I learned later that my Polish friends would rather fast than wear filthy rags. They used to barter their meager rations for clothes.

RUSSIANS used to boast about their magnificent MOTHER RUSSIA with its boundless lands, its rivers and its multitude of peoples and tribes, but whenever we asked what they thought of their rulers the majority would admit that they were tired of them. In a typical Russian manner, they would engage in lengthy discussions on religious subjects. Young men would not be convinced by us; they had one answer to every argument: "That is not true. We have been taught otherwise."

Those who were youngsters at the time of the Revolution had vague memories of a childhood spent among God-fearing people who prayed before Holy Icons and taught their children the Ten Commandments. Old men would reluctantly admit that they missed the "old days", that the Tsar "after all was not a bad man and that there was more freedom under his regime than nowadays." But they would make such risky confessions only when the young pupils of bolshevism were not present.

They all had at least one common characteristic: they were masters of pilfering and marauding. They stole all sorts of foodstuffs and would sneer at those who called them thieves. "I don't do anything wrong," they would say with unfeigned candor. "I am hungry and I must find something to eat. That's all."

If they could not find bread or rotten vegetables in the heaps of trash, they would rob their colleagues. Russians could be terribly aggressive and rude. They attacked defenseless prisoners who had some treasured possessions in their bunks.

Hunger aroused their animal instincts to such an extent that they would eat anything they found on their way: raw potatoes, potato peels. They even ate grass and weeds.

I know of a few cases of cannibalism which occurred on the trains. Prisoners crammed in cattle trains began to die from starvation. If there were among the crowd several Russians, at least one of them would cut off pieces of warm flesh and eat them on the spot.

In 1942 several bodies with the flesh of the buttocks eaten up, were unloaded at Dachau from a train that came from STUTTHOF.

Russian marauders raided the camp laboratory and devoured human embryos and viscera preserved in alcohol for German experiments. They would eat burned parts of soles, fresh paint, varnish or glue. They were indeed the only omnivorous men in the camp.

We cannot blame them. Among the Russians there were many uncivilized Mongolian shepherds forcibly enlisted in the Red Army and totally bewildered. But even those who had a high school background had not lost their heritage.

I am personally inclined to believe that the appalling behavior of some Russians in the camps was caused by their utter hopelessness. The Germans kept them in the worst possible camps and deprived them of food. Theirs was the only group that did not receive any gift parcels from the Red Cross. Russia refused to join the International Red Cross, and therefore its citizens suffered more than others who sometimes received food parcels from their relatives or from the Red Cross itself. Besides, the multitude of Russians in every German camp made it difficult to handle their problems.

Every new convoy of prisoners supplied the camp with a large amount of clothes, linen and shoes.

The richest "caravans" arrived from Hungary. It was possible to get from the Hungarian newcomers such luxuries as safety razors, soap, expensive brushes, suits and warm scarves. Hungary had not been invaded, and its population was not treated by Germans as ruthlessly as the other vanquished nations. Even when sent to a prison camp, they would not be stripped of everything that had value, as others who went through the prisons before landing in Dachau or in Birkenau. The Italians, also in a better situation, had good sweaters and warm socks. Of the Poles, only those deported after the Warsaw Insurrection of 1944 saved their civilian clothes and hats.

Russian carloads brought ragged and miserable men in tattered uniforms to the camp. Somebody said that the Russians had nothing to offer except an amazing amount of vermin. They had lost or bartered their boots for bread and tobacco and wore filthy wrappings on their feet. Their moral debasement equaled their material misery. It was dreadful to listen to the curses and dirty words used by Russian youngsters. And how they treated aged people!

However, I must admit that uncouth and tactless as they were, there was a kind of genuine fellowship and mutual understanding among them. They seldom quarreled and were on cordial terms with one another. In regard to other national groups, they remained distrustful and aloof, especially in regard to Germans, Poles and Ukrainians.

When a Russian would break the ice with you, he became a devoted and loyal friend, almost a servant. They liked music and had several gifted singers and musicians.

The Poles and Russians in the death camp proved the most stubborn and resistant group. In emergencies they would perform the tasks assigned to others. It is worth noting that the Russians in German camps received quite a lot of moral support from German communists.

On the whole, the attitude of German Nazis towards their former allies was that of a conqueror set on eliminating all undesirable elements. At the time of the victorious advance of Hitler's Armies, thousands of Russian soldiers were rounded up and disposed of with typically German pitiless efficiency.

Upon my arrival in Birkenau, I found a pathetic crowd of eighty survivors. A multitude of Russian prisoners had been shot or froze to death in uncovered enclosures. Shortly before V-Day, the Germans executed 90 Russian officers suspected of underground activities. Their colleagues, who escaped death, retaliated by killing ten SS-men on the day of liberation.

Later, when Americans took over the camp, the Russians organized several raiding parties, which robbed and murdered German landowners in the neighborhood.

A Spanish communist whom I met in a German camp said to me: "I was a Communist because I did not know Russian communism. When I got acquainted with honest-to-goodness real Bolsheviks I got fed up with communism. Anyway, I dreamed of something utterly different."

The ITALIANS, with their cheerful and devil-may-care disposition, were easily put out of gear. Many suffered nervous breakdowns. The Italians were almost as desperate as the Russians. In order to obtain a piece of stale bread, they would make knitted socks for other prisoners. I saw them rummaging among debris, looking for food. I also remember how they sang Neapolitan love songs under the windows of our block in Dachau and asked to be paid with bread.

Their beautiful country, its blessed climate and the unforgettable landscape with ancient churches and magnificent works of art, became the main topic of their conversations. With tears in their eyes, they spoke of "la bella Italia" and of the Pope who, thanks to His kindness and generosity, became a symbol of a Father of suffering mankind.

Our Italian friends were sociable and friendly, but they lacked will power. When unnerved, they lost their temper and ran into fits. That is why they often started fights with their own compatriots. SS-men thought very little of their work. They called them "d...loafers"

THE FRENCH were not held in great esteem by their fellow sufferers.

Irascible and quarrelsome, they assumed airs of intellectual superiority and would not mingle with the crowd. Almost every Frenchman was a confirmed individualist, who cared for himself and turned a deaf ear to the sufferings of others.

They had indeed brilliant minds and oratorical talents. In other circumstances, they would have been charming and interesting companions. In prison, however, other qualities were more needed. One act of charity, one friendly advice had a far greater importance than the fireworks of an intellectual discussion.

It is worth mentioning that both the Italians and the French, whose lovely countries have been for age's centers of civilization and of culture, proved an easy prey to all kinds of prison neuroses. They suffered breakdowns and went to pieces, while men and women of less civilized countries would endure dreadful sufferings with almost superhuman patience and fortitude.

In Birkenau we had a large group of CZECHS, mostly well-to-do businessmen and former government officials. They seemed deprived of any sense of humor.

Their outstanding feature was a keen interest in politics.

These solemn and dignified men would hold long talks on politics, but they were also shrewd and smart moneymakers. It was not a pretty sight to look at Czech prisoners fraternizing with German guards and ostentatiously talking only German. They hated all the Poles in the camp and would boast of their "superiority".

The most companionable and congenial were the Yugoslavs, the Dutchmen and the Scandinavians, who were extremely courteous, tactful and trustworthy.

"German Martyrs"

Each concentration camp had a certain number of German prisoners, who — if rescued after D-Day — most probably described themselves as heroes and martyrs. Unfortunately, the majority of these German-born prisoners had a long police record. They were notorious gangsters, profiteers, smugglers, gang leaders, peddlers in narcotics, deserters and prostitutes. Priests of German origin were not numerous. There was a fairly large number of German communists. All German prisoners enjoyed special privileges.

It is a sad truth that a German prisoner, even one who was mistreated by SS-men, would at a moment's notice transform himself into a pitiless executioner of his fellow sufferers. He would gladly assist the SS-guards in subduing recalcitrant prisoners and in clubbing their emaciated bodies. German inmates of horror camps were not any better than Germans outside the prison. They were the same malevolent and spiteful crowd of prospective "masters of the world". Exceptions could be counted on the fingers of one hand.

The German communists, the majority of them with a long prison record, had a well-organized underground.

A Communist plot of an uprising, projected for the day of the capitulation of Germany, was discovered by a camp leader. Instead of executing the guilty, as would have been the lot of foreign born prisoners, these German communists were transferred from Dachau to other camps and disciplinary units. According to their plan, all prisoners of Polish origin and all priests would have died in gas chambers.

Prisoners who were forced into a disciplinary squad were isolated, and could not write letters nor receive food parcels. They had scarlet labels on their overalls.

A disciplinary unit was often assigned to tasks that required superhuman physical endurance. For example, a group would be ordered to jump for hours or to carry blocks up a slippery stairway. Others were sent to a crematory to take care of the furnace or to work for 18 hours in a quarry.

The scarlet sign aroused in us such a feeling of sympathy, that whenever we met one of our less fortunate colleagues we tried to help him in one-way or another. Clothing labels bearing the first letter of the name of each country made it easy to guess "who was who", and what was his criminal record.

Chapter 11

A Journey Without End

In March of 1943 I left Birkenau with a large convoy of 1,200 prisoners. Our final destination was the camp of SACHSENHAUSEN, near Berlin. It was situated at a distance of only 25 miles from the German capital.

Transfers of prisoners from one camp to another were part of Hitler's project of mass extermination. Germans liked to scare the wits out of their victims. Prisoners hated to be sent in an unknown direction. The next camp would probably be worse than the old one. One feels better in a trap where he has already spent a night than to face a new one which holds an unknown terror.

No one was ever told where he would land.

We travelled in cattle cars for several days, without food or water. A corner of the car served as a latrine. With no blankets available, one had to sleep on the dirty floor. A prisoner who lived through the ordeal of several journeys was a hopeless wreck.

In the last months of the war, a transport of prisoners evacuated from BUCHENWALD to DACHAU contained 17 living men and 1983 corpses. The seventeen also died a few days later.

I will never forget the ghastly sight of these scrawny bodies covered with a wrinkled and livid skin. Several corpses had been partly devoured by somebody who had run amok from starvation. Locked up in cattle vans for two long weeks, without water or food, and surrounded by hundreds of dead bodies, men went crazy. Who would not — in such conditions.

Our caravan was not too bad. Only once did we have to wait in the fields under a shower of bombs, and we lost many colleagues.

When I walked into the courtyard of Sachsenhausen, it struck me that it looked different than Birkenau. Everything was neat and clean. One felt that the camp was run smoothly.

I really think that Birkenau was unique and that there was never a filthier and gloomier spot than that horrid prison.

Not long ago, I read in a newspaper that after the liberation a memorial dedicated to thousands of martyrs would be set up in Birkenau. The camp was, therefore, guarded by armed policemen; but one day they got tired of working without pay and went on strike. The next day, a man arrived with credentials signed by some high ranking official and began to remove the equipment. Eventually, the place was overrun by a crowd of plunderers, who not only carted away every piece of furniture but also dug the earth, looking for gold teeth and valuables which might have been hidden by SS-men and camp guards.

The camp where so many heroes and saints died, instead of becoming a shrine, was desecrated and trampled by gold diggers and profiteers.

Five Years or Five Centuries

I will never be able to erase from my memory the picture of Birkenau, where one year seemed a thousand years, where thousands of men and women from all parts of the world found an untimely end.

Five years seem a short space of time, but more crimes were committed during that period than during the past five centuries.

An atomic bomb is very small, but it contains enough energy to blow an entire city into pieces. In those five years more diabolic schemes were devised than in the past five centuries. Christ washing on the Cross again and again, every time His Commandment of Love was jeered at by the fiends marked with the sign of the swastika.

During those five years, Germany became an example of what might become of a people who followed the wrong path of rabid nationalism for 700 years. The germ of Nazism found an excellent breeding ground in Germany. In that country there will always be a chance for men of Hitler's type, unless the entire German nation kneels down at the feet of the Cross and makes a sine are Act of Contrition.

But there is no sign of such a spiritual rebirth.

At the time of my departure from Birkenau I noticed with dismay that only 25' men were still alive out of the total of 628 whom I met in the prison of SIERADZ. Within two months, 600 men were exterminated in the Hitlerian hell.

The surviving 25 prisoners did not last long.

Several died in Sachsenhausen from typhoid fever. Others, whose physical endurance was at the lowest, died in Birkenau. A few weeks of hard labor proved sufficient to speed their end. I am the only one who survived.

May my dear friends rest in peace, and may God Almighty grant them the eternal reward.

Sachsenhausen

SACHSENHAUSEN was a different sort of horror camp. It was too near the capital of the Reich. It was too often visited by missions and commissions and by foreign guests from neutral countries. It had to be a model camp, not a dungeon.

Eventually, we all learned that in Sachsenhausen there also were death chambers and secret rooms, where prisoners were tortured in a fiendish way. The camp had a crematory; seven large barracks served as a hospital for thousands of casualties. Yet in comparison with Birkenau, it was a wonderful place.

Our transport contained several typhoid cases. Camp authorities became panicky. The situation was made worse by the reluctance of newcomers to report their illness. We were afraid of being sent to gas chambers.

At first, no one knew that there were 300 men already stricken with the terrible fever. Twice a day a team of physicians, also prisoners, made an inspection of each block. The sick had to be removed forcibly and sent to the infirmary.

It seemed strange that the sick refused to go to a hospital. "What's the matter?" asked one of the doctors. "Why do you reject our help?"

Finally, someone answered in a whisper: "We are afraid to land in a gas chamber. It happened ever so often in Birkenau."

We then heard a long speech delivered by an intern, also a prisoner, who explained that there was no gas chamber in Sachsenhausen and that the sick would be assisted by real doctors. We listened to him with apprehension, refusing to believe.

On the same day, I fell ill and was ordered to go to the infirmary. I went there reluctantly and as soon as I saw a dark stairway leading to a public bath, I got so scared that I bolted like a frightened animal. They promptly subdued me and I was carried into a room which was indeed a real bath. The hospital was also a real one, and I found a guardian angel there, a Polish doctor, also a prisoner. He was born in Lwow, my hometown.

Thanks to his efforts and kindness, I got rid of the fever and my general condition improved strikingly.

However, though we did not see any trace of gas chambers in Sachsenhausen, and though the routine was slightly different, it was efficient as in other camps. Terrific speed, discipline and dreadful hard labor killed thousands of young and sturdy men.

After recuperating from typhus and diarrhea (Durchfal), I developed pneumonia. This time I was placed in another wing of the hospital, where three men had to share one bed. Patients died by scores. I ran away from this ghastly infirmary "for lighter cases" and reported for work. Strangely enough, in spite of the absence of medicine and treatments, my ailment left me unmarked.

In Sachsenhausen, every block had its own police and official executioners. The procedure was altogether different than that in Birkenau, where those who had some kind of authority would murder or club whomever they disliked. In Sachsenhausen, a camp leader would hand over a guilty man to the executioner. But the punishment was often worse than that inflicted by SS-men.

After a short stay in Sachsenhausen. I was sent in July of 1944 to DACHAU. Our journey proceeded in stages, we had to wait at railway stations and in various prisons. I spent several days in the largest German prison in Berlin, the famous building at Alexander Square (Alexander Platz).

In Berlin I experienced quite a disappointment. The capital of a nation that boasts of its "Kultur" had a prison which, ironically enough, was the most primitive and dirty place I could imagine —only second to Birkenau.

In three cells connected by a narrow passage millions of bedbugs had the time of their short lives. It sufficed merely to lean against the wall for a few minutes to become literally covered with vermin. And how they bit you!

I spent six sleepless nights there on my narrow cot fighting with swarms of insects. I am convinced that a longer stay in that "civilized" German prison would have made me a helpless victim of bed bugs. They would have eaten me alive.

Whenever I think of the "Kolossal" prison at Alexander Platz, a certain suspicion creeps into my mind. Who knows — maybe it was another devilish German plan to supply the cells with millions of bedbugs. Maybe they had a special bedbug farm for that purpose.

The bugs were everywhere in each prison where I had to spend a night. I was pestered by them in Halle, in Leipzig, in Hof, even in Hitler's beloved Numberg. I slept there in the same empty hall which a few years later, became the death chamber of the Nazi criminals tried by the Allies.

On July 17th, 1943, I landed in DACHAU and stayed there until Victory Day.

Chapter 12

The Martyrdom of Priests

The priests formed the largest group in each German camp. In DACHAU there were 1,600 priests (416 of

Polish nationality). They came from various countries — France, Holland, Italy, Yugoslavia, Poland and Germany.

Polish priests were persecuted for two reasons: because they were Poles and because they were Catholics.

After the invasion of Poland, German police deported almost all parish priests and members of religious communities from the regions "incorporated" into the Reich. They were thrown into prisons and later into concentration camps. In other parts of the country, regular manhunts spread panic among the inhabitants.

In his report dated January 6, 1940 and presented to the Holy Father, Cardinal Hlond, Primate of Poland, stated: "The clergy was the most harshly persecuted. Monasteries have been methodically suppressed. In many districts the life of the Church has been completely crushed, the clergy having been expelled. A great number of nuns have been dispersed. In Polish Pomerania only twenty out of 650 priests of the diocese, i.e., barely 3 per cent have been permitted to remain at their posts. The remainder (97 percent) were either shot, imprisoned or deported. It is not rare to see a priest in the midst of labor gangs repairing roads and bridges, drawing wagons of coal, and even engaged in demolishing synagogues. Some of them have been shut up for the night in pigsties, barbarously beaten and subjected to other tortures. The German persecution struck at the whole clergy from the bishops down to vicars and junior priests in small towns and villages. Bishops were beaten, insulted and forced to carry out humiliating tasks.. Incredible tortures are inflicted on those in prison. Some of the victims lost their reason..." (Excerpts from two reports; pages 328-331. The Black Book of Poland. G. P. Putnam's Sons. N. Y.)

Later on, thanks to the intervention of the Vatican, Catholic priests were kept together in one camp, namely, in DACHAU. Until 1944, DACHAU was the terminal station for all transports of prisoners in priestly clothes.

If you were to ask me who suffered the greatest hardships under German occupation, I would answer: "Jews and priests". To admit that one was a servant of God was to brand oneself as an outcast. Men who have abandoned the world for God's sake and who once prayed for martyrdom, now saw their dreams fulfilled.

They were given the worst tasks to perform: in MATTHAUSEN they toiled in stone quarries, in SACHSENHAUSEN they had to carry heavy loads from one place to another, in BUCHENWALD and in DACHAU old priests, harnessed to a roller and whipped into a run, were obliged to push it over a gravel road, sometimes barefoot. Others were forced to drain swampy meadows, to clean the gutters, or to wash the latrines and carry excrement with their own hands.

Every hour on the hour, their dormitories would be inspected by SS-men. Young dashing SS-officers, each one with a big wolf dog well trained and obedient to every command, would incite their dogs to charge like wild beasts at the priests.

Camp leaders and overseers, mostly long-term criminals, delighted in ill-treating and whipping helpless priests on any pretext. Prisoners in SACHSENHAUSEN did not hide their joy when several priests were transferred to DACHAU. "At last we will have some rest. Those poor priests seem to infuriate our guards, and everybody pays for it."

SS-men were not the only tyrants. Many prisoners, mostly communists, invented all sorts of nasty pranks in order to humiliate their God fearing neighbors.

In spite of everything, the Catholic priests with only a few exceptions, played their providential part in the grim show with dignity and supernatural fortitude to the very end.

The first stage was particularly trying, but the priests forgot their personal hardships and fulfilled their tasks as unofficial chaplains of the camps. They secretly celebrated Mass. They received and distributed Holy Communion in dark hideouts, under the bunks or on their way to work. With a magnificent contempt for their own safety, they dared to perform their sacred duties almost under the noses of the guards. Confessions were heard every day. Last Rites brought consolation to the sick and the dying.

A holy Franciscan, Father Maximilian KOLBE, the founder of famous settlements in Poland and in Japan, know as Niepokalanow, and of the widely circulated magazine RYCERZ NIEPOKALANEJ (The Knight of the Immaculate), died like a martyr.

He asked the German executioners to kill him instead of a younger man, who had a wife and small children. The strange request of the Franciscan monk was gladly fulfilled. He was left stripped of clothes in a tiny cell without windows and sentenced to die by starvation.

For two weeks, prisoners in adjoining cells heard him reciting his prayers and bestowing his blessing upon all victims of Nazi terror. After two weeks, no more strength was left in his famished body, he was still living. Finally, the German guards killed him with an injection of carbolic acid.

One of the witnesses, Brunon Borgowiec, wrote in a statement published in 1946:

"I was ordered to cart away his remains. When I entered the room I was struck with a strange radiation that seemed to emanate from the corpse. While other bodies were twisted and soiled and their faces had a dreadful 'expression of utter despair, Father Kolbe seemed to rest peacefully. He was sitting on the floor, leaning against the wall, his eyes wide open. His body was clean and radiant. One felt overcome with awe. He was a saint, no doubt about it."

Nothing could diminish the zeal of the servants of God. Not even the worst corporal punishment. They were flogged and clubbed, whenever an SS-man would catch them praying or administering the Last Rites. A priest would be savagely beaten for such a crime as hiding a rosary or a scapular. I knew a priest in SACHSENHAUSEN who was trampled to death, because a guard found a rosary in his bunk.

A priest who had been chased through one door would return by another entrance. Deprived of his rosary, he would make one of a piece of string with ten knots. It was almost impossible to obtain a larger amount of Hosts. A priest usually carried the Consecrated One on his person and distributed only very tiny particles to communicants.

German priests enjoyed many privileges. They had a special dormitory and a private chapel where, throughout the war, they could celebrate Mass. These poor frightened men were so loyal to their German bosses that the majority of them refused Holy Communion to their Polish colleagues, though with a little courage that could have been done in secret. Polish priests had to smuggle the precious wafers in a slice of bread or in paper wrapping. They entrusted the wafers to their Catholic neighbors. All these efforts and sacrifices brought a wonderful harvest. Many prisoners who never heard the Gospel, learned to know the teachings of Our Lord, thanks to these brief encounters with His servants.

I knew many saintly men who volunteered for heavy and dangerous assignments. They worked in hospitals, disciplinary camps, and the dismal steam bath where thousands were gassed. Very often, they acted as good Samaritans or guardian angels, helping or replacing those who were on the verge of complete breakdown.

One of the sublime examples of truly Samaritan activity was given by the late Msgr. KOZAL, suffragan bishop and vicar general of the diocese of Wloclawek. After two months in the prison of Wloclawek where he was subjected to various tortures, he was sent to a camp in LAD and later to DACHAU where he died as a martyr. "Prior to his arrest, he devoted himself most zealously to the service of the people of his diocese during the hostilities" (Report of Cardinal Hlond).

In DACHAU the Germans decided to punish him for two major crimes: one for being a bishop, another for carrying out his apostolic mission even in prison. He became the spiritual leader of all imprisoned priests.

After 1941 the number of prisoner-priests seemed to decline. Death was taking a terrific toll. Thousands of priests, incapacitated through overwork, died in gas chambers or in laboratories, where they were used as guinea pigs. In DACHAU 222 Polish priests were inoculated with malaria and 40 others with phlegmona, ending their lives in indescribable agony.

"The Rectory"

After 1943 conditions in some labor camps improved slightly. Discipline seemed to relax and tortures became less frequent. Prisoners could receive parcels from relatives and from the Red Cross.

The debacle of the German armies in Russia marked the first stage of a visible easing of methods.

After Stalingrad, the Germans had some misgivings as to the ultimate outcome of the war. They were crestfallen. The situation of the German army in Russia was so desperate that not even Hitler's elite, the SS-men, believed any more in the fairy tale of world domination. Many Germans were more concerned about their immediate future than about discipline.

Polish priests began to receive numerous gift parcels from Poland. All prisoners benefited from this charitable action. They now had extra rations, which the priests gave them. They also received many delicacies of which they could only dream thus far. Candy, a few raisins, were indeed a godsend from heaven.

The famous Polish author MORCINEK, a Silesian Pole who spent several years in German horror camps, describes in his book LISTYSPOD MORWY how the generosity of Polish priests saved hundreds of prisoners from starvation. They distributed bread and fats, sugar and dried fruit. They made hundreds of small packages for the sick in the hospitals and for the most needy cases in camp. The block of the priests was nicknamed "THE RECTORY" (Plebania). Long queues of hungry men, mostly Russians, waited there for bread and clothes. Whenever someone felt the pangs of hunger, he would rush to the rectory and came back beaming and pressing to his heart a piece of buttered bread or some dried fruits.

Eventually even SS-men lost their pride and began to look wistfully and pleadingly at Polish priests, or rather at their food parcels. Our former tormentors now would not risk their future for a doubtful decoration awarded for murdering of innocent prisoners or for robbing them of their possessions. For a short time at least, discipline seemed to crumble in German camps.

The same priests who a few months ago were the laughing stock of Gestapo men and of their stooges acted now almost as leaders of the camp.

The former outcasts could perform their duties openly, and they recklessly broke all the rules. It was still forbidden to celebrate Mass, but they disregarded the "Order". They preached sermons, they heard confessions and distributed Holy Communion. At first they did it stealthily, but eventually they could use the chapel installed in 1940 only for Germans. They had Novena services and retreats. The number of communicants increased amazingly. Even a few Germans would sometimes enter the chapel and listen to our songs and Christmas carols. Polish priests gave religious instruction to young boys. They tried to gain access to hospitals and disciplinary squads. One of the indomitable missionaries organized a group of Ukrainian children of Greek Catholic Faith and taught catechism while working in the stone quarry.

German communists felt insulted and frustrated. They vainly endeavored to undermine the growing influence of the holy men by sending slanderous reports to camp authorities.

A Concentration Camp Prisoner's Art of Jesus on the Cross

Sacred Heart of Jesus, carved by a prisoner on the wall of Block 11 at Oswiecim.

In one field, however, discipline did not relax until the very end, and that was the field of politics. Any kind of underground political activities was punished by a transfer to the dreaded disciplinary section.

Chapter 13

The "Puff"

In 1944 the Germans organized a brothel in DACHAU which they nicknamed the "puff. For the past four years hundreds of unhappy girls abducted by German police were forced into brothels for German soldiers. Following a new rule, the labor camps were sent several prostitutes for their disposal. At first, only prisoners of German origin were permitted to visit the "puff. Later on, all men could enter the barrack where several girls brought from the woman's division were enslaved and supervised by "old hands" with criminal records. The house was situated at a certain distance from the main settlement but quite near the block occupied by priests.

Some prisoners who remembered the terrible plight of their owns sisters and wives forced by Germans into prostitution were indignant at first and organized a boycott of the "puff". But eventually the temptation proved too strong. The Catholic priests tried hard to counter act this evil influence. They dissuaded young boys from frequenting the "puff". They even organized a sort of picketing of the house of "white slavery".

The "puff" was opened only in the evening. We had informers who reported on those who had "registered". Shortly before the arrival of the "guests", hundreds of prisoners would gather at the entrance of the "puff", greeting every guest with boos and catcalls. Processions of prisoners used to follow those who left the house, shouting at them and spitting in their faces. The best result was obtained by spreading rumors that SS-men would liquidate for laboratory tests those who frequented the "puff". This peculiar sort of boycott proved so successful that only a few men dared to challenge the crowd. They finally gave up, because they became a target for cruel jokes and insulting remarks.

Here again, because of the impending doom of Hitler's armies, the SS-men would not use all their power and decided to compromise. Almost all the "white slaves" were transferred to another camp.

In 1945 conditions in DACHAU became again unbearable. Typhoid fever was rampant. Not a single food parcel reached the prisoners for several months. Devastated Poland, overrun by Red Armies, could not help its children any more. The spectre of hunger made its appearance.

The camp of DACHAU had to accommodate hundreds of prisoners evacuated from endangered areas. Germany was no more an impregnable fortress. Its walls were crumbling under the impact of bombs. The Day of Wrath was approaching.

In a block where 600 men lived in narrow bunks, first 1,500 then 2,000 had to find a place to sleep. The communal laundry was already too small for the thousands of bundles of filthy rags. Only an insignificant number of prisoners could use the communal bath and get rid of lice. DACHAU was then almost as filthy as BIRKENAU and we were literally being eaten by vermin.

Each day new transports of men, stricken with typhoid fever had to be sent to the hospital which soon proved inadequate; epidemics were spreading at an incredible speed. Half of the settlement had to be isolated and fenced in with barbed wires.

DACHAU was another replica of HELL.

Starved and delirious, the sick refused to stay in their bunks and ran wildly all over the enclosure. Every day 100 to 300 corpses were removed from the dormitories. Old timers, who had lived through other harrowing experiences, began to break down. The hospital staff lost almost its entire personnel. The few guards and SS-men who survived could not handle the situation.

No one listened to the frantic screams and pathetic moans of the sick. The dead lay in the bunks for several days. In some instances, the guards left them in their bunks on purpose, in order to use their rations. In such a case, the "corpse" was listed as "critically ill".

The air was filled with the stench of decaying bodies, piled up in the yards, on the road, and in the blocks. Close to the crematory, a mountain of corpses swarmed with maggots.

The threat of impending disaster left the authorities of the camp dumfounded and helpless.

In those days, no one really cared for the prisoners. The SS-men were concerned only with their personal future.

When a feeling of despair took hold of all of us, one of the SS-men began to shout hysterically: "Let's ask the priests to do something. They will be able to keep the blocks under control."

He was right. The priests lived up to expectations. They did not reject the opportunity to perform heroic acts of charity, and joyfully entered the isolated barracks where no one dared to go. They cleaned the filthy quarters, where thousands of stricken men waited for death. They fought for a cup of water, for dressings, for medicine that would bring solace to mangy bodies covered with festering wounds. Many priests contracted contagious diseases while taking care of typhoid cases. Those who replaced them continued to bring relief and encouragement to the hopeless and the broken-hearted.

Some of the prisoners were opposed to this magnificent action. Too many priests were murdered already. "The war will end soon", they said, "Our fatherland will need you." You have no right to commit suicide now, when freedom is almost at the door."

A note of protest sent to the priests was left unanswered.

Hundreds of good Samaritans paid with their lives for their generosity. Many died on the eve of liberation, but they certainly did not regret what they had done for their brothers, remembering the words of Jesus Christ:

Come blessed of my Father, take possession of the kingdom prepared for you from the foundation of the world; for I was hungry and you gave me to eat; I was thirsty and you gave me to drink; I was a stranger and you took me in; naked and you covered me; sick and you visited me; I was in prison and you came to me.

Poles are often praised for their indomitable spirit. I would like to add: Poland is a heroic nation but the real spiritual leaders of its people are the Polish priests!

There were, of course, isolated cases of moral surrender and of abasement even among priests. Men who lacked a real vocation soon threw off the mask of goodness, showing their evil selves, but the majority won the respect of all prisoners, even of those who had no faith.

Out of a total of 1,600 Polish priests, 860 died in DACHAU like martyrs. American soldiers who entered the Camp found only 750 clergymen. (The total casualties among Polish priests in German camps exceeded 1,263.)

Many priests released from DACHAU returned to Poland. A large group is still busy among the Displaced Persons in Germany. They deserve a lot of sympathy. For two years they did not receive any kind of support from UNRRA. They were viewed with disfavor and animosity. Transferred from one camp to another in a most discourteous manner, they never failed to bring relief and spiritual consolation to their dejected countrymen. For obvious reasons, a great number of priests could not return to their fatherland. Having been persecuted not only by Nazis but also by communists, they would have to end their lives in prison or in Siberia. These men will be homeless for years to come, only because they love God and their fatherland.

They Could Not Cry

Someone asked me whether we cried all the time in those dreadful camps, or whether we had fits of despair only occasionally. I stared at him and began to laugh. "We never cried", I answered him. "There is a limit to tears. When you have suffered too much, you have no tears left."

And that is the truth. In normal life almost everyone expresses his sadness by tears; in the camp a crying man was an unusual sight.

I heard less complaints and less sorrowful confessions in DACHAU or in BIRKENAU then in the world prior to the war. Prisoners gradually lost the ability of expressing their sorrow. During the four years spent in concentration camps, I saw only two men who really cried.

One was a youngster, a Jew in BIRKENAU, and the other was an Italian, who begged with a tearful voice that his garments be returned to him. He suffered from exposure and had been stripped of his clothes as a punishment for a slight misdemeanor.

I often listened to screams. I heard the heart-rending gasping of strangled men, but that had nothing in common with what we call "weeping". It was the sound of a suffering animal.

In Cracow, in the prison of Monteluppi, my cell was close to the dark dungeon where recalcitrant men and women were kept for several days for questioning. Hunger, darkness and terror were used to break down their resistance. In that secret room invisible martyrs moaned and screamed for help. For many days and nights I heard the terrifying groans and yells of some unfortunate woman, who was finally silenced by SS-men. I saw her body carried away by prison guards.

When a prisoner was flogged, and he usually received from twenty five to seventy five strokes with a rawhide whip, he would howl and scream for hours but that was not what we call "crying". To cry in a horror camp would be a waste of time. Instead of arousing sympathy, it would drive the tormentors and guards crazy and incite them to more cruel excesses. If they saw a crying man, they would get into fits of anger, like a wild beast excited by the sight of fresh blood.

The only emotion we knew was fear. Our shattered nerves reacted in a different way than that of normal human beings. Agonizing pain makes the heart bleed but deprives one of the capability of crying. One becomes dumb like a block of stone.

I often meditated about the Sufferings of Our Lord, and I wondered that the Son of God, who shed tears when He predicted the doom of Jerusalem and Who cried at the death of Lazarus, had no tears to shed during His own Martyrdom. The Mother of God also did not weep while standing at the foot of the Cross. Why? I found answers to these puzzling questions in the German concentration camp.

Being myself rather prone to tears, I never cried while in prison.

A friend of mine, Mr. Radzik, was forced to witness the ordeal of his son, a boy of eighteen, who was dragged to the gas chamber. He did not cry, he only grew frightfully pale. But later on, in Frejmann near Munich where we met after liberation and talked about the past, he burst into tears like a child.

Ignacy Balinski, the well known Polish statesman, wrote in his diary that he thanks God for the special grace of "dumbness" bestowed upon the victims of persecution. After having endured excruciating tortures, prisoners gradually became insensible to further experiences. Their brains and hearts seemed to freeze or petrify. One becomes partly blind and deaf. Unable to think, unable to perceive and understand what is going on.

All those who spent several years in prison would certainly confirm Balinski's statement. They suffered from temporary amnesia or lapses of memory. Some of my friends could not remember the first name of their father or brother. I saw prisoners who upon returning from the labor camp could not find their own bunk; others would not be able to remember the address of their parents or their own home. One of them, instead of giving the accurate description of the street where his wife lived, wrote down the number of the house where she used to dwell with her family as a child.

After several months of continuous subjugation and coercion, the sturdiest men became as thoughtless and weak as earthworms. Without any reason, they would expose themselves to beatings or would let themselves be trampled to death. They would drowsily loiter around heaps of rubbish and would eat the most repulsive and unpalatable leftovers.

I saw prisoners forced into trucks which would bring them to gas chambers and, though they knew where they were being sent, they would not utter a word of protest. They would depart smiling like someone going on a pleasure trip. I saw dying men leaning against a wall mashing crumbs of bread, apparently unaware that they were approaching the most important hour of their lives.

The range of suffering is as extensive as that of human emotions.

God Is Peace

Elias, fleeing from the wicked Jezabel, went out into the desert, where he was ready to die that he might no longer be witness of the miseries of his people. But the angel of God appeared to him and gave him food, and by the strength of that food he walked forty days, till he came to mount Horeb, where he had a vision of God. As the Lord approached, He was preceded by a strong wind which rocked the mountains and broke the rocks in pieces; but the Lord was not in the wind. After the wind came an earthquake, but the Lord was not in the earthquake. And after the earthquake came a fire, yet the Lord was not in the fire. Finally there came a sighing of a gentle air, and behold the Lord was there.

God is in peace and in tranquility, in the sweet flowing song or music, in the prayerful attitude of people in church, in acts of kindness and works of mercy, in duty and work well done.

God is Order and Harmony. You would vainly look for Him where hatred and pride destroy the Divine Order, bringing chaos and despair.

I am often asked what was the attitude of the prisoners to religion.

In times of calamity, when we are threatened by an impending disaster, we often turn our eyes to the skies and we call on our heavenly Father. Who does not remember the slogan which circulated among GI's during the last war: "There are no atheists in foxholes".

It would, therefore, seem logical that inmates of horror camps would be inclined to place all their trust in God. Unfortunately, that was not the case.

Only where there is a spark of hope does one plead for assistance, but where no hope is left men of little faith become the prey of despair. Those whose faith is deeply rooted have one prayer only: FIAT VOLUTAS TUA! — Thy will be done!

In BIRKENAU, no one would even dream of a possible escape or of a better future. There was no future and no hope for anyone. We often spoke in a casual way of our "journey's end" in a crematory. Death was our constant companion. We got used to it.

Men, who knew that their hours were counted and that they might appear before their Maker at any time, did not give Him another thought. Many pronounced His Name with bitterness and with anger.

"If there is a God, why does He allow such crimes to be committed?" "Do you really mean that God is Almighty — mighty lazy, that's what He is!" one prisoner said to me. "You say that He is merciful? Maybe so, but He is merciful only towards our tormentors. "He knows and sees everything. Well! He must be pretty shortsighted!"

How true are the words of the Psalmist:

"Shall any one in the sepulcher declare Thy mercy: and Thy truth in destruction?" (Psalm 87, 12)

Often, when a ghastly crime was being committed in our presence, the prisoners would ask me with a sneer: "Father! where is your God?"

I do not blame my unhappy friends, who never tried to pray and who would rather carry on idle and superficial conversations than discuss the most important subject.

The worse our condition, the less we talked of religion. To mention religion was to touch an open wound. Most of the time, an ironic and malicious smile would be the only reaction.

Gustaw MORCINEK in a book entitled LETTERS FROM ROME relates the story of an evening in DACHAU.

"At nightfall, the prisoners would listen to the noisy and deafening music carried by a powerful loudspeaker.

"Suddenly, the boisterous medley of Wagner's works was interrupted by the voice of the German announcer, and we heard the soft and soothing melody of Schubert's AVE MARIA. And all at once something very strange happened. All the prisoners stopped talking and stood spellbound, staring at the loudspeaker.

"Suddenly, the boisterous medley of Wagner's works was interrupted by the voice of the German announcer, and we heard the soft and soothing melody of Schubert's AVE MARIA. And all at once something very strange happened. All the prisoners stopped talking and stood spellbound, staring at the loudspeaker.

"We were no more in the courtyard of a horror camp, but in the brightness of a Heavenly dawn, at the feet of our Queen among the angels and saints.

"But a few minutes later, the gates of the camp broke open and a column of slave workers marched in, escorted by guards and overseers. The SS-men rushed to the exhausted men, who hardly could lift their swollen and bleeding feet. As usual, the guards kicked and clubbed those who moved too slowly. Curses and screams drowned out the music.

"The spell was broken."

"The same men who a few seconds ago, had soared on the wings of the enchanting melody to Paradise felt more dejected and forlorn than ever before. The gentle melody was a mockery. We could not stand it. We rushed inside the barracks, cursing and sneering. The deadly poison of unbelief crept into our hearts."

Every unpunished crime we had to witness caused a violent reaction against the Omnipotent but seemingly indifferent God.

One of my neighbors often begged me to "save him from unbelief." I tried to share with him my own faith in God's Justice, but after a day or two he would return in a state of gloomy confusion. It proved a difficult task to preserve our faith in an atmosphere of damnable depravity and malevolence, amidst notorious killers who were rewarded for their crimes.

Only one prisoner in BIRKENAU came to me to confession. As I have said before, conditions in SACHSENHAUSEN were less appalling than in BIRKENAU and therefore I had many penitents there. They were all comparatively in good condition and did not suffer as much as the others. During my stay in the hospital, where I spent seven weeks among half starved and worn out "casualties", not a single man asked me to hear his confession, but at night a few interns used to kneel at the foot of the bed and ask me for absolution.

"For hell shall not confess to Thee neither shall death praise Thee: nor shall they that go down into the pit, look for Thy truth. The living, the living, shall give praise to Thee." (Isaiah 38, 18-19).

Dachau was an accursed place where religious feelings were totally stifled. Only when conditions improved in the face of the impending doom of the German armies, did prisoners slowly begin to return to God. They prayed and went to confession. This was also due to the influence of the numerous priests in Dachau. In general, however, I saw hundreds of breakdowns but I witnessed only a few conversions.

All these experiences helped me in solving, at least partly, the riddle of Russian atheism. I do not believe any more that Godless propaganda, the antireligious attitude of the rulers, and persecutions wholly account for the great number of agnostics in Russia. It was rather the ruthless police system, with its labor camps where human beings slowly deteriorated, and the incredible poverty of millions of Russia's citizens that weakened the people's faith in God.

Let me quote once more from the writings of MORCINEK, who after his liberation went to Rome and "walked from one church to another seeking God." He called his pilgrimage an escape from unbelief. "I could not find God in horror camps. I could not see His Face there. I saw only thousands of piled up human bones, I saw misery and debasement and vermin. I could not hear His Voice in the deafening choir of groans of my fellow sufferers who were dying in mud and snow, under fences and in filthy bunks.

"I could not hear God where only curses and shouts broke from the lips of human beasts.

"I lost God in a cloud of dark smoke which hung over the crematories.

"I lost Him in the scarlet mist of human blood, in the foul stench of rotting human bodies.

"I lost Him in a crowd of Jobs covered with ulcers.

"I am endeavoring to find Him in Rome amid white marble columns and in churches resplendent with gold.

I am entering one church after another, trying to find God..."

Morcinek found Him in the Eternal City.

It seems that faith and hope and piety need an atmosphere of normal and harmonious life.

A Camp of Death is a place where the natural order is constantly violated.

Those whose faith was only a part of their paternal heritage but was not deeply rooted in their hearts, manifesting itself only on "Holy days" — their faith would burst like a soap bubble on the threshold of the prison. Sometimes it would sway in the wind like a reed, at times soaring high up to heaven or sweeping the ground.

The ones who possessed real faith now had an opportunity to appreciate its meaning. It manifested itself in the darkest hours of their lives, giving them incredible endurance and helping them to get through the narrow passages of suffering.

Horror camps became a testing ground for Catholics. Many bad Catholics upon liberation promptly chose the path which leads to perdition. Others had only one desire: to become servants of God. They entered seminaries and convents. There are many prisoners who lost their faith, but who feel unhappy and desperate without it and endeavor to find their lost treasure. If they err, they at least deserve to be called men of good will.

Abyssus Abyssum Invocat

When asked by God what he desired most, King Solomon asked his Maker to make him neither too wealthy nor too poor. "Give me neither beggary, nor riches: give me only the necessaries of life: Lest perhaps being filled, I should be tempted to deny, and say: Who is the Lord? or being compelled by poverty, I should steal, and for-swear the name of my God." (Prov. 30, 8-9)

Hunger and misery are loyal allies of the devil; he likes to tempt those who have no strength left in them and have reached the end of their rope.

Hundreds of honest men who would have felt insulted if someone had told them that they would become petty thieves or pickpockets, after a long stay in concentration camps lost all restraint and became regular thieves.

Prompted by hunger, they would steal bread and leftovers. They would even rob their neighbors. To have an extra slice of stale bread hidden in one's tattered clothes was enough to make a prisoner feel better, less despondent.

It became an obsession. It gave him a semblance of security.

He would touch the piece of bread from time to time, only to see if it was still there. During the night, he would hide it under his pillowcase filled with straw. Whenever he woke up, his first reaction was to make sure the bread was not stolen.

It was not an easy task to find a good hideout for such treasures. A prisoner would watch his neighbor for days, and when he discovered the hiding place, he would wait to rob him when the owner fell asleep.

It did not bother him that his victim may have needed that stale and moldy piece of bread more than medicine, and that to deprive him of the few extra calories would expose him to dizzy spells during work.

In our camp, we considered this kind of petty stealing a major crime. The guilty, when caught by colleagues, would be ruthlessly punished. Some bread stealers were bludgeoned to death by their comrades. In Sieradz, a man who stole a loaf of bread had both arms fractured, all his teeth knocked out, and almost lost his sight.

Hunger is an evil counselor. Adult prisoners, when driven by hunger, would behave like thoughtless children. They ate anything they found. Many died, because they swallowed rotten food, though they knew well that they were killing themselves. I remember a man who received a food parcel from his relatives for the first time. He ate all its contents at once. A few hours later, he was taken ill and died from a dreadful cramp.

Hundreds of prisoners literally committed suicide by a reckless or imprudent attitude. They would get shot, because they turned their heads while on roll call. They knew well that they would be shot for such an act, yet they committed it.

Gradually, we all became so hardboiled that neither natural nonviolent death would stir us. We saw too many bloody spectacles, with SS-men killing innocent victims. We got used to the sight of corpses. We slept among them, we walked over them. A living or a dead man — what's the difference, anyway. We all were only half alive. And for the German executioners to kill a man was as unimportant as to crush a mosquito.

After a few years spent in concentration camps, the prisoners themselves began to toughen. Lynching was a daily occurrence. A prisoner suspected of disloyalty towards his friends would be speedily disposed of. He would be mugged and murdered in some dark nook or in a stone quarry. No one was ever punished for such a "trifling matter". When someone told on a killer, SS-men would rub their heads and sneer: "Another dog is gone."

In BIRKENAU, two former Polish policemen were strangled by their colleagues, who remembered that they were unfair to an arrested man prior to the war. In DACHAU, in the dormitory occupied by Russians, lynching was indeed a daily occurrence.

Convoys of prisoners transferred to other camps were often the scene of dreadful executions. The SS-men who escorted the prisoners in the closed cars were practically cut off from the outside world for many days. They were at the mercy of their prisoners. These locked cars became regular traps for our tyrants. Many SS-men lost their lives during these dangerous assignments.

Chapter 14

Words That Kill

We seldom realize the importance of words. A kind word may heal a deadly wound, a harsh word may kill the strongest heart.

The German used the filthiest slang when addressing prisoners. German officers with college education and uncouth soldiers all behaved in the same manner. They never called a prisoner otherwise than "you swine", "you dirty dog". And these words were the cleanest and kindest in their repertory. Curses, disgusting and shocking expressions, were poured like stinking water upon our heads.

Later on, a vile kind of slang became the "language" of the inhabitants of the horror camps. Only older men and priests showed sufficient will power to refrain from using it. The youth was badly contaminated by it. Teenagers would organize contests for the dirtiest nicknames.

The Germans, Russians, Italians and a group of Polish schoolboys from Lodz used the vilest language.

One of the signs of the moral deterioration of the inmates of the death camps was the total indifference with which prisoners would rob their dying comrades of their clothes and shoes. When a man collapsed and would not regain consciousness for several minutes, prisoners would begin to fight for his clothes. If the man came to his senses and begged them to leave him in peace, they ignored his moans. Disrobed and left naked, he had to die from exposure.

Old and young, grandfathers and grandsons, all got used to walking in blood. Concentration camps robbed men of their conscience, turned their hearts to stone, made beasts of human beings.

Immediately after V-Day, the liberated prisoners (KACETY) were sent to special camps for refugees. Shortly after, they gained the reputation of being the toughest element among displaced persons. The spirit of revenge took hold of them, and they could not restrain themselves in manifesting their hatred for Germans. They would organize raiding parties and stickups. They did it with complete contempt for their own safety.

Reckless and thoughtless, they would violate all rules and expose themselves to death or imprisonment.

Former inmates of horror camps gladly volunteered to track down war criminals. They handed them over to Allied authorities.

Some of them were religious, but they regarded their faith only as a component and manifestation of patriotism. They were attached to religious customs which were part of their daily life in their own fatherland, but they rejected all that hampered their lower instincts. Loafing and tramping were their favorite exercise. The KACETY could not get rid of evil influence left by the camp atmosphere and were a public nuisance for quite a long time after liberation.

Many former prisoners developed all sorts of neuroses. One of them would hide slices of bread and was suspicious lest his neighbors would deprive him of his treasure, "set aside for a dark hour".

While I was waiting for my emigration visa in 1946 in Frankfurt am Main, I met a Brazilian citizen of German origin in a transitory camp for prospective emigrants. He used to look for food in all wastebaskets. This man received twice as much to eat as others, but he suffered from a constant fear of starving to death.

It will take a long time to heal all the wounds and to readjust the crippled hearts and twisted minds to a normal life. Many former victims of Nazi terror will certainly become valuable citizens, as soon as they get rid of the specter of their horrible past.

Hatred and Love

God has given us a powerful remedy for all social ills.

It is Christian Love. Without Love, this world would crumble to pieces. Without love and charity, life would disappear from our globe.

Thanks to love, millions of human beings were saved from the hell of war. It was love that prompted men of other faiths to save the lives of thousands of Jews, who would have otherwise perished in gas chambers.

Thanks to Christian charity, hundreds and thousands of prisoners of war withstood the hardships and the monotony of a six year imprisonment, and hundreds of men persecuted for their political convictions were helped to escape from concentration camps.

Horror camps became centers of conflicting elements: of Hatred and of Love. The horrible wounds inflicted by the beastly "Masters of Europe" were healed by the wonderful ointment called MERCY. Among devils you met angels.

I wish I could write another little report on my own experiences, in which I might tell you of the many acts of charity by my colleagues to which I owe my life!

It was not easy to be charitable in a German camp. On the other hand, there was never a place where Charity had less trouble in finding out who needed its consolation. It was not easy to share with your neighbor a rotten potato or some cabbage leaves without attracting the attention of the German guards, who hated everything that reminded them of God, of His teachings, and of goodness.

To approach a dying man meant to incur a dreadful punishment. One would be kicked and clubbed pitilessly. Instead of assisting others one would promptly become a helpless victim, himself in need of help.

It was not easy to smile, when one felt desperate and sad, or to say a kind word when your own heart ached badly. It was not easy to feed a starving friend when you had to eat grass and bark, or to give him a drink when your parched mouth was bleeding from want of water. It was hard to drag a friend, who had collapsed in the midst of the road, and to hold him up when your own arms were thin and weak, like those of a starved child. Beggars had to give alms. The starved had to feed the starving. The blind had to lead the blind.

Often charity caused the untimely death of some poor man, who received the heavenly gift of water but who should not have drunk it. Both men were aware of it, but the sick man would plead and beg for a drop of water, and his comrade would not have the courage to refuse it. Similar tragedies occurred when someone begged for food.

The American GI's who arrived at Dachau before the Germans had time to gas all their victims, were so appalled at the crowd of men resembling skeletons more than human beings, that they treated them to unusual amounts of food. They opened the barracks where all the food was stored and allowed the liberated phantoms to take their full share. The entire stock of canned foodstuffs vanished in no time.

A few hours later, dismayed American boys had to take care of hundreds of victims of deadly cramps. Their stomachs could not digest food. After a starvation diet of several years, one square meal became deadly poison. And thousands of martyrs who had escaped the gas chambers did not live long enough to enjoy their freedom. They died by scores.

In other instances, a freezing man would beg you for a rag.

You knew that this piece of soiled clothing was vermin infested, as were all our garments. You knew that the lice were carriers of typhus, but the man was livid. He shivered and groaned and clutched at your arm with numb hands that were covered with sores. You yielded and gave him the warm wrap, only to repent later because it became a shroud for the poor fellow.

Once we found a dying friend in the fields. Merciful prisoners took care of him. They lifted him from the ground and stealthily placed him in a warmer nook. After work, they brought him into the camp. He was still alive, but during the roll call we had to place him with the other sick men. It was bitterly cold. He got a fit of shivering. He moaned and whimpered, drawing the attention of a guard, who quickly sped his death with several savage blows. And as he wanted to make sure that "the dog" would not come to life again, he trampled upon his emaciated chest with heavy, nailed boots.

It would have been more merciful to leave our colleague in the fields, where he would have died in peace.

Never before did charitable souls have so many puzzling problems to solve.

Hearing confessions or administering the Last Rites also was punished severely. Priests, however, found in their faith a source of strength and fortitude. They never hesitated to bring solace to the sick and dying.

"Organized Relief"

Very often, an ailing man who was unable to go to work and was left behind would receive some extra food gathered by a friend during the day — a potato, a rotten tomato, a few cabbage leaves.

We called it "organized relief".

If it was discovered it was severely punished by the SS-men.

It can be truthfully stated that in spite of the deterioration of ethics, the inmates of the concentration camps performed heroic acts of charity. I knew men who would share every bit of their food with others. There were several prisoners who made it a habit to share their bowl of soup with those who were more hungry. I saw men tearing their own miserable scarf in two to provide a friend with warm wrapping.

Most of the men suffered from malnutrition. Here again Charity found a beautiful field of action. The healthier men helped the sick; the ingenious and clever advised the helpless ones. A famous professor had to be taught how to use the shovel. Many former officials and diplomats felt completely puzzled by their new occupations. Those who lived in cities had to learn how to till the soil.

A newcomer soon signed his own death sentence if his neighbors did not acquaint him with the rules of the camp. He usually did not believe that he would not be allowed to rest for a few minutes during a strenuous assignment. But when he attracted the attention of an SS-man, both he and his companions would suffer equally from cruel reprisals. In BIRKENAU, the SS-men carefully noted the names of men who tried to get a little rest at work, and the next day the "criminals" would be sent to a gas chamber.

When a man sat down, all the others were on the lookout. If one of them noticed an approaching guard, he sent a swift warning which alerted the whole team. The "loafer" promptly joined the squad and everyone sighed with relief.

There is nothing I dislike more than regimentation.

One of its most unpleasant products are the "queues". This kind of "order" was invented and imposed upon by totalitarian dictatorships. I would rather not receive anything than wait for something in a line. These queues will always remind me of prisons, of horror camps, of captivity. However, queues in a horror camp were a must.

We had to wait for bread, for coffee, for a bowl of warm soup. There were queues in front of the communal bath, and in front of the latrine. Prisoners had to live and die in queues.

Charity found its way even here: younger and stronger men would give their places to the aged and the infirm. They would cheer one another with jokes and with words of encouragement.

Nowhere else is the power of the word so great as in a camp of Death. Some words crushed our will to live, others healed our wounds and brought relief. Evil words crept into the camps and made their way to each one of us, but good words repaired the damage and restored our faith in justice.

A kind word proved in many cases more valuable than a loaf of bread. After all, material help brought relief only for a few hours. The next day would be as gloomy and hopeless. HOW LONG? —That was the question which seemed to rack our brains.

To make a hopeless case feel better, it was sufficient to bring the man some "good news", real or invented. When we heard that the situation on the fronts was "improving", which meant the impending doom of Hitler's armies, we appreciated this news more than bread and butter.

Our News Service

There was no barbed wire strong enough to prevent news from reaching us in every dormitory. We knew what was happening on the battlefronts, but we kept the bad news for ourselves. The good news was quickly transmitted to the sick.

If we had nothing to tell, we would invent wonderful news. We called it "parole". It was kind of whispered News service. Thanks to it, many prisoners pulled through their worst hours.

Even those who did not live long enough to greet their liberators had their last hour made brighter. They knew at least that their families would enjoy the V Day of Freedom.

LIFE IS HOPE — this ironic saying of Oscar Wilde never proved more true than during the war. Without hope, all European nations would have become victims of despair. Without hope, the Poles would have not been able to live through the German occupation.

It is a pity that deeds of Christian Charity and acts of Love seem to occur more seldom than crimes dictated by Hate. Good Christians do not boast about their kindness, mindful of the Teachings of Christ Who said: "Let not your left hand know what the right hand doeth."

But it is a consoling thought that Christian Love has not been wiped out by godless wars.

I am often asked whether we were completely isolated from the world, and invariably my answer sounds unbelievable: "We knew everything and our news service was more efficient than you think."

In fact, we knew what was going on not only in Europe but also in America and in other parts of the world. We followed with interest the development of the Balkan campaign, the war in Russia, the invasion of Africa and of Italy, as well as the crossing of the Channel. We knew the number of planes that were shot down and the number of the prisoners of war. We received descriptions of the siege of Stalingrad, the insurrection of Warsaw and the battle of Monte Cassino. We knew when the Allies landed in Normandy and when they crossed the Rhine.

We got this news through various channels and by various means. It should be remembered that in each camp there were thousands of former politicians, newspapermen, teachers, diplomats and social workers. Many among us were sent to prison because we listened to foreign broadcasts, or because we took part in underground activities. We had several expert commentators too.

The prison window was an excellent observation post. We looked through it not only at the clouds, but we also read news of political importance through the windowpane. A speeding hospital train, along column of armored cars rushing at a terrific speed, fighter planes, a caravan of horse carts loaded with furniture and refugees, a truck with wounded German soldiers — everything was "news" and everything was commented on and explained.

The window sometimes disclosed hair-raising scenes.

In Cracow all prison windows were partly covered with a screen, but I once saw a Gestapo man molesting a prisoner. He kicked the old man and incited a bloodhound to jump at his throat. All this was done in order to force the man to carry a huge stone to the top of a pile of coal. The man stumbled and fell several times. He tried vainly to chase the dog who tore his miserable overalls and bit his thin legs.

I stood there behind the screen, utterly helpless, stirred by the ghastly sight, when a bullet brushed the frame of the window, missing it by a fraction of an inch. The SS-man spotted me and decided to liquidate an uninvited witness. I bolted and crouched under the window, waiting for death. But no one entered the cell.

As for news — we also got it whenever a group of guards would gather in the narrow passages and engage in lengthy discussions. We tried to stay near the door and catch a few words, which would form the basis of our daily reports. Thus we learned of what was going on at the various fronts, of their mounting hardships and growing fears.

In some of the camps loudspeakers were installed and official news from German fronts was announced each day. It was biased, of course, and distorted, but we learned how to separate the grains of truth from the chaff of propaganda.

A rich source of information was to be found in every new trainload of prisoners. After a while, our new comrades would feel more confident and would share with us their information.

Several hundred prisoners had to work in factories and on farms situated at some distance from the camp. They mixed with civilians who often spoke freely of the war and the political situation. Upon their return to the camp, we were showered with exciting reports.

The administration was directed by SS-men and German officials, but a certain number of prisoners who seemed more submissive would be employed as office workers, helpers and janitors. They swept the floors, washed the windows, they took care of the stoves. I heard that in some instances, during the absence of the "boss", a prisoner employed in his office would promptly get hold of the radio set and listen to broadcasts from London or from other countries. It happened seldom, but we valued more than anything else information brought by an invisible voice, from the other part of the world.

Skilled mechanics, electricians, radiomen and engineers had to work in their capacity, unless they were considered thoroughly unreliable and deserving to be punished or liquidated. A man who was called to repair a radio set would never miss the chance of listening to foreign broadcasts. Even SS-men were helpless when amid discordant voices, thanks to the ability of the mechanic, the loud and distinct voice of a British commentator would for a while drown all other noises and bring wonderful news of victorious battles or the number of German casualties in the space of a few seconds.

We had among us fearless men who dared to construct their own radio sets. And what extraordinary little gadgets they would make out of nothing. A tiny but most efficient radio set was placed in a small box, easy to conceal. There was a guard of Polish origin, a really good man in BIRKENAU. He helped us a lot. One day his German colleagues found a radio set in his bunk. A few hours later, the man was on his way to the dreaded camp of AUSCHWITZ (Oswiecim). I never heard of him since.

A few prisoners pretended that they were friendly to the SS-men. They praised the German army and expressed their admiration for Nazi commanders. An SS-man would listen in silence, nodding his head, but gradually he would feel more confident and would engage in a real discussion. He would even admit with a sorrowful look that things were not as good as they seemed and that such and such a commander had a difficult time with those d... enemies, the British, so that finally news of real value would be obtained by the not too loyal collaborator.

SS-men sometimes disclosed important news by their behavior.

For example, after the unsuccessful attempt on Hitler's life, discipline in the camps became unbearable. All the supervisors and SS-men were more watchful and vigilant than ever. They walked as though on springs, with the arrogance of typical German Junkers. On the other hand, a grim and despondent looking SS-man who seemed to forget his duties — had more than likely been thrown into that state by gloomy news from the front. And it usually meant that the German armies had taken a terrific beating.

As far back as 1943, one of the high-ranking SS-officers rushed into our cell and started a terrific brawl. He ordered all the prisoners to lie down on the floor, and jumped and ran around, shouting wildly:"Alle Polen Und Englander Ausrotten!" (Kill all the Poles and Englishmen!)

The same day, the news of the German attack on Yugoslavia spread all over the prison.

We often got hold of German newspapers. The real news was to be found between the lines.

Where there is smoke there is fire. During our work in the open, no one could cover the skies, and the skies became another stage on which momentous events were displayed. Whenever we saw squadrons of German or Allied bombers, we used to make bets and guesses. When only Allied planes soared over our roofs, and not a single German fighter or pursuit plane would chase them, we felt inwardly elated. We knew that the German Air Force was disintegrating under the impact of Allied bombs.

Leaflets thrown by the Allies on cities and villages reached us quite often. They were cautiously circulated in dormitories, but we waited until nightfall to read them.

After 1940, in DACHAU, after the lights were out in the Polish section of the dormitory the voice of a political commentator would be heard by a group of prisoners.

One of them was on the lookout and would warn us if a guard was approaching. The task of that "whispering commentator" was that of gathering all gossip and rumors and to prepare a short summary with his own predictions. He usually began with bad news, but each report had a happy ending and the prisoners went to sleep with some hope.

It was quite an art to collect the news and circulate it, and some prisoners achieved a sort of fame for their ingenuity.

In my first letter sent to my parents after liberation, I told them that all my previous messages from the camp were just a pack of lies. And this is a fact. It was forbidden to describe our life in camp; we could only repeat one sentence: "I am in good health. Conditions are good." A few meaningless greetings would end the message.

I AM IN GOOD HEALTH — that was the letter I sent to my parents when I was almost starved to death. The same kind of a message reached them at the time of my critical illness, when, stricken with typhoid fever and later with pneumonia, I waited for merciful death to end my sufferings.

Hundreds of letters reached the addresses after the death of the prisoner. A mother must have been greatly perplexed when she received two letters on the same day, one announcing that her son had passed away from heart condition, and the other one containing the pleasant news that he was in excellent health and was receiving fine treatment in camp.

At first, prisoners tried to write a little more, but their letters were thrown into the wastebasket, or were filed and kept for further questioning by German censors.

On the whole, it proved much easier to obtain news from the outside than to send out a truthful letter.

Later on, we learned how to smuggle letters through strangers, whom we met on our working assignments. SS-men gladly accepted bribes and although they seldom fulfilled their promises, some of the messages would finally reach the addressee. But of course, no prisoner would ever trust an SS-man and his letter would contain cryptic information about another person. For example: "I heard from uncle Joseph that Julius (that would mean the prisoner) is very ill; he suffered a nervous breakdown. He won't eat, and the doctors think that he will die. "A father or mother, guided by an infallible instinct, understood the real meaning of the postcard.

Chapter 15

The Last Act

After the downfall of Germany, the entire country seemed to fall apart. Cities and towns burned like bonfires. Railway stations and bridges, highways and tracks were showered with bombs. Germany was being blown up. Transportation means were nonexistent. Thousands of American planes swarmed above the countryside.

Panic-stricken crowds of refugees, prisoners of war, and wounded soldiers pushed their way along the roads and highways. The grim picture of the September debacle in Poland during 1939 was now repeated in Germany.

The same chaos reigned in DACHAU, where the confusion was increased by the arrival of prisoners from other camps. Hunger and typhus were the only masters. No one seemed to care what would happen to the prison camp. The SS-men and guards were now concerned only about their own immediate future.

During the night, we heard the thunder of heavy artillery and we literally counted the hours between us and Victory Day.

Suddenly, the news of our transfer to a camp in Tyrol spread like fire. It sounded incredible. No one believed it. A few men got hysterical at the thought of another excruciating experience.

A few hours later we learned the truth.

Our blocks were promptly cleared; all men were ordered to gather in the yard and be ready to depart "in an unknown direction".

Thanks to God, the camp was already in a state of complete disintegration. Prisoners milled wildly, but thousands obeyed the orders. All the German prisoners and a small group of Russians appeared in the yard and were sent "somewhere". All the others remained in Dachau until the very end. Camp authorities were too panicky to handle the situation and the comparatively small number of guards was unable to round up the demoralized crowds.

On the 27th of April a cold rain drizzled, and we were not sent to work. It was a good sign.

Around noon, we heard the warning sound of the siren. It meant that armored cars were patrolling the countryside.

A stampede of scared SS-men and overseers was the first signal of our V-Day. My heart beat so fast that I could not breathe.

Not one SS-man was in the camp. But there were still several watchmen in the towers guarding the approach to the settlement.

The siren ceased. The silence was alarming.

We were puzzled and unable to make any decision. An hour passed, and suddenly a detachment of SS-men marched back into the camp.

During the night, I noticed one of my neighbors, a Polish priest, sewing a small Polish flag.

On April 28th the weather was fine. Hundreds of American and British planes seemed to fall in reckless dives, but after releasing their bombs on the railway station of DACHAU and on other strategic points they soared up high to heaven.

Never before did I see so many smiling faces.

At noon, a wild shouting burst from thousands of throats:

"AMERICANS! AMERICANS!

The first detachments were rushing in the direction of the camp, across the fields and the plantation. Prisoners who had strength enough climbed on the roofs. Others broke down and wept for the first time, loudly like children. Strangers hugged one another. Some one began to sing his national anthem.

Then an ominous silence fell on the camp.

We later learned that untimely enthusiasm was aroused purposely by German provocateurs, in order to increase the general chaos and speed up a mass liquidation of all prisoners. We also learned later that the inhabitants of DACHAU who had heard the terrific uproar created by the wind thought that a revolt had broken out in the camp.

It was the first time that SS-men did not move a finger to maintain order. They felt too despondent, knowing that they might be punished as ruthlessly for their crimes as we had once been for trifling matters. A white flag had already been hoisted on the building of the administration.

The next day was for us THE day. The RED LETTER DAY which will never be erased from our memory.

Freedom

It was Sunday, April 29, 1945.

Even the weather was perfect. It seemed that nature itself wanted to appear at its best: clad in flowers, and streaming with gold. I never saw such a lovely Spring day in my life. Even the horror camp with all its filth and stench did not look dire. Even the faces of dying men seemed to smile.

After Mass, I walked along the main street of the camp. Everyone who still could walk was there, looking at the sky and pointing cheerfully at the planes.

I heard a muffled sound of machine guns.

Could they be so near? It seemed impossible. But the rattling of the gun sounded louder and louder. At the end of the road some shooting was going on.

I almost collapsed from joy, when I saw white rags and handkerchiefs fluttering like birds on the watchtowers.

"That's it. SS-men are giving up. It is the end!" we shouted wildly.

And suddenly a small fellow in an American battledress and a helmet appeared from nowhere at the barbed wire fence.

We stared at him with unbelieving eyes.

An American? Alone? Could it be that he is patrolling? Is he bringing us freedom? An American in this death camp of corpses.

The multitude of ragged men looking like specters stared in silence at the little soldier. Many sick men got up on their feet and stood swaying, their eyes wide open and almost blinded by tears.

Freedom was standing at the threshold, and we were unable to move. No one believed what he saw.

Only after a long while, when another soldier and then another approached the camp, and when later a jeep filled with GI's alighted at the gate, one wild scream burst from all lips:

"AMERICANS!"

Strangely enough we simply did not know what to do. We felt that we had to react, to say something, to do something. Maybe to tear the barbed wire to pieces or to run wild. But we stood there dumbfounded and petrified with joy.

Our bewilderment did not last long.

Someone started running, and that was the signal.

No one who has not been in a concentration camp has ever experienced our elation. No one ever saw such a hysterical crowd of men who almost lost their minds from joy.

Hundreds of men climbed on trees and roofs, shouting at the top of their voices: "LONG LIVE AMERICA. LONG LIVE FREEDOM."

The windows of the isolated blocks and ambulatories burst open, and spectral faces and scrawny arms appeared in the frames. The sick and the dying crawled on their hands and knees, many without clothes on their skinny bodies, others covered only with rags.

Leaning on walls or supported by stronger comrades, a procession of staggering, frightening skeletons made its way through the crowd. Some of them found enough energy to walk as far as the fence and express their joy in meaningless sounds.

Prisoners from various blocks greeted one another. They laughed and cried: many sang their own national anthems.

A few minutes after the arrival of the American soldiers, a commanding officer made his appearance at the main entrance. He found there a group of prisoners, a delegation formed to greet the liberators. The American officer listened to them and then dropped on his knees and loudly recited the Our Father in broken German. "We must thank God for Victory," he said later.

The other soldier who entered the camp was an American newspaperwoman in battledress.

The camp was in an uproar. Prisoners shouted and cheered wildly. Some of them endeavored to tear down the wooden gates and to cut the wire fence. The net of barbed wire almost burst under the impact of the excited crowd. Several prisoners ran out of the camp. They hugged American GI's; kissed them and patted their faces.

Appalled by the sight of famished men, they gave up their own rations and looked horrified at the staggering prisoners who gulped the food like starved animals. They would fight for a can of meat, pushing one another and falling on the ground.

Others began ransacking neighboring houses. With a few exceptions, they all returned to the camp. Only communists and accomplices of the SS-men took advantage of the chaotic conditions and ran for their life, for fear of revenge.

On the roofs national flags were hoisted. The first one to appear was the Polish flag. Next rose the Czech flag. Later, dozens of flags like multicolored flowers swayed in the wind. They were made in secret, weeks ago.

Te Deum Laudamus.

It was 5 P.M. Ten minutes later there was not a single SS-man on the lookout. Twenty SS-men were shot on the spot; others were escorted to the assembly point for German prisoners of war.

Before the arrival of Americans, the Russians rounded up the SS-men in one of the watchtowers and murdered them with their own weapons. The guards in the second tower were shot by Americans, because snipers attacked the GI's in spite of the white flag. All the watchtowers were torn down, and the camp was taken over by military authorities.

Two hours later almost all the barracks had their own radio sets.

In the chapel, the liberated priests intoned the TE DEUM.

The night came — the first unforgettable night of freedom. In the flickering light of bonfires, human shadows roamed around. Hundreds of prisoners looted the warehouse and cooked an unbelievable concoction of foodstuffs in the open. An overwhelming elation took hold of everyone. We were confident that real freedom had arrived.

Scrawny weaklings on wobbly legs joined the exhilarated crowds. They tried to sing, but their voices sounded hollow and weird. There was real joy in their sunken eyes, however, and a smile on their pale lips.

No one paid attention to the corpses lying beside the merry bon-fires. We had gotten so used to death. The main thing was that WE lived in spite of typhus, in spite of clubbings and floggings, in spite of the organized terror of the SS-men and their accomplices.

The American GI's brought us Freedom on the butts of their rifles. They opened a common grave and thousands of ghosts were being brought to life.

On that memorable night no one could sleep.

The world was resounding with the thunder of guns. Sometimes the old fear crept into our hearts. Sometimes old nightmares would disturb our peace. But when dawn came, we were again confident and utterly happy.

Very early in the morning, an international committee headed by a Pole, Mr. Kokoszka, took over the camp.

The first meeting of the Committee was carried on in an atmosphere of understanding and fraternal solidarity. All motions were adopted unanimously. After all, the members of the new Committee knew one another and they knew every one's record.

They were still shaky and exhausted. They had dizzy spells, but they felt wonderful.

There was only one thought and one wish: to help everybody. That was their task. To save those stricken with mortal diseases and those who still had a chance to live. We all wanted to work and to help, to prepare ourselves for ultimate return to our beloved fatherlands.

And, indeed, all former victims found in themselves enough energy to make a new start immediately. The former prisoners, aided by the American soldiers, gladly cleaned up the filthy hospital. They disinfected the wards; they helped in preparing injections. The corpses were removed, mountains of rubbish disappeared in no time. It was not an easy task, but joy proved to be a powerful motor, and we were all leaping with joy.

On the 3rd of May, which is the Polish National Holiday, the Poles celebrated it in a solemn and inspiring way. A procession of Polish prisoners gathered in the courtyard. At the foot of a gigantic Cross an altar was placed. The oldest priest in the camp said Mass and delivered a beautiful sermon.

The entire community took part in the celebration, with national groups displaying their own flags. In the same courtyard, where not long ago the most revolting show in the world was on, now a triumphant Thanksgiving service was being held. Hundreds of colorful flags swayed gaily in the breeze.

The next day at 10 A.M., a Memorial Mass was said for the American soldiers killed in action. And again, all national groups and a guard of honor composed of American GI's took part in the service. Late in the evening, a service for the repose of the souls of the Dachau martyrs attracted all the former inmates and became another inspiring manifestation.

Chapter 16

Souvenir Hunters

In the meantime, our camp was overrun by thousands of tourists who rushed from all parts of Europe and the globe: diplomats, high-ranking officers of Allied Armies, foreign correspondents, representatives of the press, film and radio personalities. Interviews were uninterruptedly carried on. Photographers took snapshots of every spot and of the liberated victims.

The crematory with its piles of more than 2,000 corpses attracted the curiosity of thousands of newcomers. Crowds milled around the dismal temple of modern Moloch. Everybody was anxious to see the dreadful mountain of decaying bodies.

A group of tourists visited the railway station of DACHAU, where thousands of corpses shipped from BUCHENWALD, were piled up in two railway trains.

Men and women would not believe that this was not just a nightmare. It seemed incredible to them, that in modern times a civilized nation could have committed such barbarous crimes and attained the depths of such utter debasement. But what they saw was only a pale reflection of reality.

They saw only dead bodies. They saw the mute weapons of crime, traces of footsteps of victims and their tortures. They did not see the "factory of death" in action.

It was like the famous museum of Madame Tissot in London, with its wax figures, petrified and unable to express any emotions except the final one, that of dismay.

They did not see SS-men whipping and strangling their victims.

They did not see wolfhounds tearing the flesh of half starved prisoners.

They did not see the funeral pyre in the forest with its dead and living "fuel", burning like an immense torch.

They saw only mountains of ashes. They did not see the fire.

No one realized the agony suffered by the inmates of the horror camps for days and weeks, for months and years.

All the pictures taken after V-DAY in DACHAU are only obituaries.

No one will be able to guess the thoughts and the feelings of those who spent so many frightful days and nights in DACHAU and in other camps.

A Narrow Escape

At the time of liberation, the Seventh American Army found 32,000 prisoners, including 10,0000 Poles, in the camp at DACHAU.

Not all the liberated survived: thousands died after regaining freedom. Typhus and other contagious diseases took a heavy toll even after V-DAY.

I am fully convinced that those who survived owe their survival to a miracle. Like other camps, ours too was to have been completely liquidated, allowing no one to escape alive. Instead, this is what actually happened.

A few days after the arrival of American troops, a document was found in the offices of the camp. It contained a sentence of death for all of us. It was an order issued by Himmler for two camps, that of DACHAU and that of FLOSEENBURG. The order was an answer to the question made by the commanders of the camps, whether they should surrender the camp to the Allies.

April 14, 1945. SURRENDER OUT OF QUESTION. THE CAMP MUST BE IMMEDIATELY EVACUATED. NOT ONE SINGLE PRISONER SHOULD BE CAUGHT BY THE ENEMY. PRISONERS BEHAVED IN A HORRID WAY TOWARDS THE CIVILIAN POPULATION IN BUCHENWALD. Signed: Himmler.

Not one of the Dachau prisoners was to have survived. All were to have been exterminated on the eve of liberation. There is no doubt about it.

Captured SS-men confessed that all inmates of the camp were to have been liquidated in the following manner:

On April 29th on Sunday, at 8:30 P.M., a roll call was to take place in the main courtyard. During the roll call, German bombers would set fire to the camp. All prisoners were to be machine-gunned or killed with hand grenades, so that no trace of the horror camp would be left. SS-men hidden in watchtowers (10 men in each one) and 400 others quartered in the barracks intended to start the "show".

This plan was substantiated by the great amount of weapons found in all the watchtowers: bullets, machine guns and grenades.

Sunday night, one division of Storm Troopers was also on its way to the camp, probably to carry out the sinister project, but was repelled by the artillery barrage of American tanks.

Americans had only a few tanks. They were, in fact, only patrolling the countryside; but in spite of this, they succeeded in paralyzing the German forces and in liberating the martyrs of DACHAU.

When we saw the sentence of death, meant for every one of us, we forgot that Himmler was now powerless. All the elation suddenly left us and gave place to gloom and fear. Dazed and shocked, we could not rejoice any more. Only after a long while, we realized that we had again had a narrow escape.

It was indeed a miracle that the diabolical plan was frustrated.

I often think of the coincidence which brought about the liberation. A small detachment of American soldiers happened to be sent to the railway station of DACHAU, where they saw two trains filled with human bodies. They decided to investigate further.

On their way, they saw other corpses piled up in ditches and in the woods. They noticed that all wore similar clothes. It looked like a collection of prisoners from some concentration camp.

They did not know anything about the camp of Dachau; but they began to inquire and several German farmers told them there was a concentration camp in the neighborhood.

Without asking their superiors for permission, they pushed forward and made a search. It was against immediate orders and had nothing to do with the general strategic plan of the Allied commanders. In fact, the American Seventh Army intended to occupy DACHAU only the next day. It was a miracle that a small team of American GI's had initiated their own strategy. They took over the camp and guarded it, until the arrival of reinforcements.

Thus, three hours before the projected massacre, the monstrous camp was overpowered by a small detachment of valiant American boys.

That WAS a miracle.

The final stratagem of the Hitlerian horror show, the execution of 32,000 prisoners, was scrapped.

We owed this to good St. Joseph. In a solemn Novena, the camp was dedicated to the Patron Saint of homeless refugees and victims of persecutions. Saint Joseph rescued us from the fangs of Hitler, as He rescued the Holy Babe from the hands of Herod.

Supermen

In May, 1945, the former inmates of DACHAU began to return to their fatherlands. They used every kind of available transportation: cars, trucks, bicycles and planes. The first to depart were the French, the citizens of Luxemburg, Belgium and Holland. Later on, larger groups of Czechs, Jugoslav's and Russians left the infamous place.

At the end of May, only the Poles remained in Dachau. In June they were transferred to the old barracks once used by the Storm Troopers at Frejman near Munich.

At first, it was intended to set fire to the camp for fear of epidemics, but eventually another suggestion was accepted, that of sending all German war criminals to DACHAU. Our bunks were now occupied by SS-men, and camp guards were chosen from among former victims.

The SS-men deserve a special mention.

Hitler's devoted zealots, the famous Storm Troopers, formed the elite of Nazism. These young men, brought up in special institutions, blindly followed the doctrine of National Socialism. They were fed on the imperialistic and pagan theories of Rosenberg and Goebbels, and became worthy successors of the German "Raub Ritters" and the Knights of the Cross.

While the Knights of the Cross converted the heathen population of Prussia and of Lithuania to Catholicism, using methods very much like those applied 700 years later by the Gestapo, the Storm Troopers despised Christian ideology as being inadequate for the purposes of the Master Race. They were either agnostics who rejected any kind of faith in God, or they practiced ancient Germanic heathenism, based upon the ancient German pagan hero worship. These fanatical disciples of Hitler, brought up in schools for prospective executioners, were taught the most revolting methods of subduing the recalcitrant patriots of invaded countries.

According to Hitler's program, the German Reich had the glorious future of becoming the ruler of the world. All nations were to follow its doctrine of the Supremacy of the State and to serve as obedient subjects or loyal satellites of the Reich. The German Race was to assume the responsibilities of the supreme ruler of the world. All members of the Master Race were "supermen", while other nations were composed of slaves born to serve an autocratic Germania. Jesus Christ and His religion of Love and brotherhood were rejected. Only the worship of proud and pitiless Germanic deities was worthy of "supermen".

The German youth, inoculated with these principles, became amass of cold-blooded, brazen and cruel SS-men, imbued with hatred and greed, blindly obedient to their Master — "The Fuehrer". Hitler-jugend organizations spread all over Germany, like a net of dangerous gangs. Hitler had no difficulty in choosing tormentors and spies, Gestapo agents, SS-guards and fifth columnists.

All the positions in social services were entrusted to Storm Troopers. SS-men were sent to the front or were ordered to supervise concentration camps. Gestapo men became the bosses of the department of justice, of all tribunals and prisons.

These men in uniforms, with the ominous sign of the swastika and the dead skull on their caps, were the real builders of "Greater Germany". Armed with guns and whips, they forced into submission all independent and active opponents.

Hitler could count on his "elite". The SS-men never failed in carrying out their bloody assignments.

They were trained in special "schools" (e.g. at the sinister Fort VII — in Poznań) how to torture prisoners, how to buffet them and lash them with cowhide whips, how to kill them with rifle butts and clubs. They were taught how to break ribs and legs, how to tear nails, how to smite women on the breasts with rubber pipes, and —how to do it quickly, efficiently and "with a smile".

They had every chance to practice such tortures as the famous "air pump" on helpless victims. (A rubber tube was inserted into the anus and air was pumped with a bicycle pump into the bowels, often causing internal rupture).

The trained Gestapo men who left these schools "with honors" were sent to the various countries invaded by German Armies. According to reports published in the "Black Book of Poland" (Putnam. NY), the Gestapo men were recruited mainly from Berlin and other Prussian provinces; few of them were Germans from the Southern Provinces.

An SS-man who got his diploma from a college for killers was indeed an expert in the art of slaughtering. When he wanted to strangle a man, he would jump on him like an infuriated wild beast and break his ribs with a few crushing blows. He was a master of gymnastics; he could leap and run at top speed.

Many SS-men lost every semblance of humanity; they were personified devils indeed.

When an SS-man was too lazy to do his job, he would order his well trained mastiff to replace him. These dogs obeyed their masters and seemed to enjoy biting and tearing into the flesh of their victims. Sometimes a dog would be more "human" than an SS-man and refuse to torture the wretched body which lay on the ground in a pool of blood.

The infamous Jung, a dashing young officer of the Storm Troopers, enjoyed murdering women. He would shoot girls, but before executing them he would rape each one and then shoot her in the stomach, in order to prolong her sufferings. He would stare at the writhing body with an expression of sadistic delight.

Another "old hand", the aged SS-officer Betcher, cynically admitted in public that he was the worst "pig" in the camp and that he himself shot thousands of prisoners for his own pleasure. Shortly before liberation, he executed 90 Russian officers.

We had a famous German scientist, in DACHAU who was also a zealous Hitlerite. He came from Berlin to direct research work in the camp laboratories. His name was Dr. Schilling. With complete disregard for ethics, he used helpless prisoners as guinea pigs; he inoculated 1,100 healthy men with malaria. Others like Dr. Schultz inoculated scores of others with phlegmonous boils which caused a dreadfully painful deterioration of tissues.

These worthy disciples of Hitler committed despicable atrocities every day. They performed excruciating operations on men and women, to whom they refused any kind of anesthetic. They killed prisoners with gas and with poisons. We never heard of a nervous breakdown among our executioners.

Ferocity and pitilessness were lavishly rewarded. The most bloodthirsty SS-men attained the heights of their career at top speed. They were granted decorations and special allowances. The higher the rank of an SS-man, the darker was the record of his past deeds.

It seems almost unbelievable that several thousand prisoners blindly obeyed a comparatively small group of guards. In fact, one SS-man could subdue an entire company of slave workers. A long column of prisoners, stretching for miles, was only a line of wooden puppets, which could be pushed into a pit with one powerful blow. One SS-man was able to throw us out of gear, or spread panic, like a hound among defenseless rabbits. He could kill anyone or as many prisoners as he liked.

The SS-men were as evil as their super-leader, the man who set fire to the world. Exceptions to the rule were so few, that it maybe stated without exaggeration that all SS-men were criminals. They were symbols of Godlessness, a living example of the debasement of human beings who replaced Christian Love with Hate and Pride.

"Deutschland, Deutschland Uber Alles"

Hitler and his close friends probably never surmised that their methods of education would bring such infernal results, that it was possible to degrade and twist human souls to such a degree.

One of the war criminals, the former governor of Warsaw, Frank, said before dying on the gallows in

Nuremberg; "We never thought that forsaking God would bring such appalling results."

The German state with all its wealth and natural beauty reached the depths of misery and despair in its downfall. We must remember that a nation which boasted of its "Kultur" and its small number of illiterates bears a far greater responsibility for mass murders than a backward country like Russia, where the words of Christ on the Cross can be applied to thousands of people: "They know not what they do."

The Germans knew only too well what they were doing.

After my liberation, I went to Munich. I felt lost and perplexed amidst ruins and rubble. I could not find my way, and I asked a German woman if she knew a place called Freimann, where former prisoners were kept in a camp. She showed me the way, and, as we walked along the same path, we began to talk about DACHAU.

The woman looked shocked and amazed upon hearing of the horror camp. "I did not know anything about it," she interrupted me. "No one knew anything about prison camps."

I looked at her a little startled.

A few days later, other Germans tried to persuade me that it was the first time in their lives that they had heard of horror camps.

Ironically enough even Germans who served as Storm Troopers tried to make us believe in their total ignorance of mass murders.

Can we accept their confession as "bona fide"?

After the liberation of DACHAU, when German farmers from adjoining villages were called to cart away the corpses for burial in a common grave, they expressed their amazement and dismay. Some of them were on the verge of collapsing, others cried loudly. They obviously were more than puzzled. Is it possible that they really have been kept in complete ignorance for years?

In Kalisz during the trial of a Polish underground patriot, German prosecutors refused to believe that he did not know of the radio set installed in his apartment. I would not have believed him either. He could not have been unaware of the existence of a noisy radio set in his own dwelling.

I do not believe and cannot be convinced that the Germans were unaware of the concentration camps and of the ignominious treatment of innocent victims. Only very naive people may swallow lies offered them by culprits who desperately try to look innocent and "white as snow".

The German people KNEW what was going on. This statement can be substantiated by a number of facts.

In the concentration camps there were hundreds of German communists, German criminals and German priests. They suffered and died in the same way as the others did.

Thousands of Germans were employed by the administration of the camps. They could roam freely in the countryside. They made trips to towns and villages. They had relatives and friends to whom they spoke and boasted of their experiences. Even if we admit that they kept quiet, we cannot forget that numerous artisans and skilled workers were called by camp authorities to make repairs. These men returned to their homes after work. We met them quite often in BIRKENAU and in DACHAU. They knew the plight of the prisoners quite well.

Concentration camps were situated in the vicinity of cities and villages. Passers-by often met long columns of underfed and ragged prisoners, bearing marks of torture on their faces and hands.

Transports and trucks with prisoners clad in striped clothes were seen by inhabitants of country places and cities. Long processions of captured men and women were often driven through streets or herded at railway stations.

Millions of Germans had the opportunity to witness the pathetic crowds. Millions of Germans got acquainted with the dismal picture of swollen faces, covered with blisters and wounds. Millions of Germans saw the clouds of smoke which at night rose from the chimneys in numerous crematories and from funeral pyres in the woods.

The salvos of execution squads and the rattling of machine guns were audible to the inhabitants of surrounding farms.

Every day post offices transmitted hundreds of cables announcing the death of prisoners. After all, post office employees also had relatives to whom they talked after work. They were not bound by any pledge of silence.

SS-men had their living quarters outside the camp. They went into restaurants, into bars. They certainly did not keep silent all the time. And many went home on leave. Moreover, many of them carried on their persons snapshots of naked tortured prisoners, or of the torture chambers.

It would be more honest and more convincing if the Germans would admit that they KNEW but that they were afraid to raise their voice in protest, knowing the fate that would befall them and their relatives. But their pharisaical attitude is, indeed, despicable!

"We Are Not Guilty"

Only in Schwanheim, a suburb of Frankfurt am Main, did I meet a few Catholics who felt guilty and ashamed of the crimes committed by their compatriots. They tried to atone for the sins of others, by helping former prisoners. But these were isolated cases. The majority of Germans are convinced that they should not bear any responsibility for a regime installed by a group of Nazis. They react violently to the opinion that a civilized nation that has tolerated mass murders is responsible for them.

"We are not guilty", they keep on repeating. "It was Hitler that waged the war. All the crimes were committed by SS-men, by members of the Gestapo, by members of the Nazi party."

If we admit that genocide was committed solely in concentration camps and that the only guilty ones were members of Hitler's party, the SS-men and Gestapo officials, we must remember that these SS-men and Gestapo executioners were sons of German families. They were brought up by German mothers. They were chosen from among Germans who had not a drop of foreign blood. They were the ELITE, who enjoyed privileges because of their typically German background. The entire nation was proud of these boys, selected by "The Fuehrer" to represent the German spirit at its best.

And they were not an insignificant group. Hundreds of thousands of German youngsters were trained as future SS-men. Every third family in Germany had a son, or a brother or a husband in the Gestapo or the SS-troops.

Horror camps were not the only places where genocide was committed. In the East, millions of Russians and Jews were put to death in public executions.

In the camps for labor workers, millions of kidnapped slaves from all parts of Europe were forced to build up the war potential of the Reich. Each village, each factory, had hundreds of slave workers, whose plight was often as heartrending as that of the inmates of DACHAU. They were also forced to perform dangerous and heavy-tasks; they were also flogged and abused and starved by their overseers.

Whenever a new transport of slave workers arrived in a village or in town, there was a stampede of prospective bosses, who rushed to the market place to choose the strongest men and women. Who was it that compelled nine-year-old children to work in mines and forests? Who was it that depraved their souls and forced them to forget their native tongue? Who spied and shadowed and denounced thousands of men and women for the slightest misdemeanor? Who collaborated with SS-men in prisons and hospitals, where genocide was adopted as a daily routine?

How can we say that all these mortal sins were committed only by a few party men?

When we were driven from the railway station of HALLE to the prison, German passers-by gathered on the sidewalks and laughed and sneered at us. I remember how we were abused and insulted by German women, and how German children threw stones and mud at helpless victims.

Were they all SS-men?

When Hitler waged the war and the Germans listened to thousands of innocent victims. Speakers which carried his boisterous and screaming voice, who was it that applauded and cheered the beloved "Fuehrer" frantically? Only members of his party?

Twenty million human beings were murdered by the Germans. They were not war victims; they were victims of a hatred cultivated by the German nation. One hundred million human beings were oppressed and subdued, not by the spirit of war but by the spirit of German pride.

Even a hundred thousand Nazis would not be able to perpetrate all the crimes. Without the support of the nation, the Nazi Party would not have been in a position to realize its program of genocide.

Atrocities were committed by the army, by the police, by the administration of the entire country, by the majority of industrialists and by thousands of farmers — in a word, by Germany. And that is why the German nation ought to atone for these unbelievably fiendish offenses. That is why the world must not permit that these brutal and outrageous conditions be ever repeated in the future.

Moral law teaches us to defend the victims of injustice. The Germans knew what was going on in the countries subjugated by them. It was sufficient to read their papers, full of vivid descriptions of the methods applied to crush the resistance of freedom loving nations. But they never raised a voice of protest. Those who tolerate injustice committed in their presence are also guilty of crime.

Hitler was the Number One criminal. His stooges and party men share the responsibility with him, but the nation as a whole is guilty of endorsing and approving his devilish program of mass murder.

Where there is guilt, there must be punishment. Atonement for sin becomes a lesser burden, when we admit our guilt and accept the consequences. Instead of pleading innocent and complaining of harsh treatment, the Germans should listen to the wise advice of Monsignor Francis Woznica former Vicar General in Katowice (Silesia).

Msgr. Woznica was expelled from Upper Silesia and sent to Germany. In a pastoral letter he wrote as follows:

We will accept our plight. As a punishment for the sins of those who committed grave offenses against the Polish Nation, against humanity and against the most sacred Laws. We will accept our sufferings as an Atonement for our sins, committed when we cowardly kept silent, as well as for all the crimes committed by the National Socialist rulers of which we are also guilty. Though we feel bitter, we will not cultivate in our hearts hatred towards other nations and particularly towards the Poles.

The German nation was misled by the false light of Nazi doctrine. Like migrating birds which smash their heads on a light tower, the Germans are now paying for their appalling mistakes. Those who have trampled upon the Law of God and all human rights are now being trampled to death amidst the ruins of their cities and churches.

It is a lesson for all of us, for the entire world.

Any nation that builds its future on the false foundation of egotism and pride, depriving others of liberty, sooner or later will crumble into ruins. A house built on sand is doomed from its very beginning.

The Unfinished Symphony

We often forget that the war was won not only by armies but also by the civilian populations of the occupied countries. Children and adults, men and women, the young and the aged contributed to the common cause by their indomitable courage and unselfishness.

There were many heroes among the soldiers of the allied armies, but there were equally great heroes among schoolboys, among civilian workers and farmers, among housewives and young girls in all the subjugated countries.

Those who had no weapons undermined the strength of the enemy by sabotaging his war effort and organizing passive resistance. In subjugated countries millions of human hearts constituted millions of insurmountable obstacles.

Concentration camps were another battlefront in the interior of Germany. Millions of prisoners required thousands of guards. Young strong men who could have served in the army were sent as SS-men to camps, weakening the military potential of the Reich.

The crimes committed by the Germans challenged God's patience, but the sufferings and sacrifices of the martyrs were speeding God's intervention. If the blood of one innocent man, Abel, stirred the Heavens, then surely the blood shed by millions of innocent people also cried to Heaven for vengeance.

The Polish nation lost the greatest number of children on the three battlefronts. However, those who survived have still to wait for ultimate victory. Thus far, the harvest of V-Day has been wasted. There is no Peace on earth, and millions of prisoners are suffering martyrdom in horror camps in another country which also has forsaken the Golden Rule, forcing countless multitudes into slavery.

Countries sold out and betrayed are still waiting for liberation. Poland has been refused the fruits of victory.

My friends, citizens of other countries, have long ago returned to their fatherlands, which enjoy real freedom. The Poles have been liberated from one enslavement only to fall under another yoke, as ruthless and godless as Nazism. Polish refugees are tramping foreign lands, their dreams of a free and happy Poland shattered. Poland today is not the land of which we dreamed in our prison bunks; nor is it the one for which we fought on the battlefronts and died in prisons.

Five hundred thousand former Polish soldiers, the first to fight against oppression, are now refused the harvest of victory. They are undesirable exiles. Their deceived and homesick hearts are pining for Justice and Freedom. We all pray for it with the words of the Polish poet: GIVE US BACK OUR FATHERLAND AND OUR FREEDOM O LORD!

Only in Christ and through Christ can there be real brotherhood, justice, freedom and peace.

How to Contact The Author

Originally published in 1944, A True Account Of Life in a Concentration Camp. Remade and translated by World War II Publishing from Man's Inhumanity: A True Account of Life in a Concentration Camp, by Father Melchior.

Glenn Langohr remade this book from the public domain to give a voice to the voiceless. If you would like to check out Glenn's other books on Amazon, they are available in kindle, print and audio book worldwide. He writes prison memoirs, prayer books and self help books, along with remade public domain works.

Dear reader,

> It is with sincere gratitude that I would like to thank you for reading Auschwitz Survivor: How I Survived Hitler's Ovens. I truly hope this book has been an eye opening experience. If you have enjoyed this book, **please consider being kind enough to leave a review on Amazon.** It would be helpful to other readers and me. Tap this link and scroll down about halfway on the left to where it says, want to leave a review~ If you can share it on Facebook, Twitter or anywhere else I thank you and will gift out a FREE kindle copy of one of my other books! Or, If you want one of my other books and can't afford it, I will gift you a kindle book. I write prison and drug war books, and prayer books. You can contact me at rollcallthebook@gmail.com or friend me on Facebook to keep up with updates and praise reports here~ https://www.facebook.com/glennlangohrcalifornia

Would you rather listen to my books? Here is a complete list of my audio books~
http://amzn.to/1aeliPs

God Bless You.

You can contact Glenn:
Author Page: http://www.amazon.com/-/e/B00571NY5A
Author Page UK: http://www.amazon.co.uk/-/e/B00571NY5A
Blog: http://www.audiobookprisonstories.com
http://rollcallthebook.blogspot.com/
Smashwords: http://www.smashwords.com/profile/view/lockdownpublishing.com
Twitter: https://twitter.com/#!/rollcallthebook

Printed in Great Britain
by Amazon